VEGAN YACK ATTACK
ON THE GO!

VEGAN YACK ATTACK
ON THE GO!

PLANT-BASED RECIPES FOR YOUR FAST-PACED VEGAN LIFESTYLE

JACKIE SOBON

FAIR WINDS

Brimming with creative inspiration, how-to projects, and useful information to enrich your everyday life, Quarto Knows is a favorite destination for those pursuing their interests and passions. Visit our site and dig deeper with our books into your area of interest: Quarto Creates, Quarto Cooks, Quarto Homes, Quarto Lives, Quarto Drives, Quarto Explores, Quarto Gifts, or Quarto Kids.

First Published in 2018 by Fair Winds Press, an imprint of The Quarto Group, 100 Cummings Center, Suite 265-D, Beverly, MA 01915, USA.
T (978) 282-9590 F (978) 283-2742 QuartoKnows.com

Fair Winds Press titles are also available at discount for retail, wholesale, promotional, and bulk purchase. For details, contact the Special Sales Manager by email at specialsales@quarto.com or by mail at The Quarto Group, Attn: Special Sales Manager, 401 Second Avenue North, Suite 310, Minneapolis, MN 55401, USA.

22 21 20 19 18   2 3 4 5

ISBN: 978-1-63159-422-9

Digital edition published in 2018

Library of Congress Cataloging-in-Publication Data

Sobon, Jackie, author.
Vegan yack attack on the go! : plant-based recipes for your fast-paced
  vegan lifestyle / Jackie Sobon.
ISBN 9781631594229 (hardcover book)
1. Vegan cooking. 2. Cookbooks.
TX837 .S678 2018
641.5/636--dc23
LCCN 2017059560

Design and Page Layout: Think Studio | thinkstudionyc.com
Photography: Jackie Sobon

Printed in China

This book is dedicated to those who are actively trying to improve their quality of life through the food choices they make.

CONTENTS

INTRODUCTION

When I first went vegan, nearly seven years ago, I worked full-time as a design engineer in a boring office with a boring lunch room. I wasn't really into cooking at the time, and I was buying freezer meals for lunch and snacking on chips and cookies. But, freezer food was pretty pricey for what I was getting out of it, and that ultimately started me on my path to home-cooking.

For the first month or so, I was looking up recipes and packing them for breakfast and lunch, on the go. Then, looking up recipes led me to researching about quality ingredients and where my food was actually coming from. Bless the internet for being the rabbit hole that it is because it was not long before I decided to go vegetarian. And, a couple months later, I went vegan. I just could not deny the facts about the effects of animal agriculture on climate change, the effects of animal products on health, and the treatment of workers and animals in factory farms.

After that, I was in a pinch. Back then, vegan freezer meals were not a thing, so living on frozen food was definitely out. So, I ate mostly raw food at work because it was super easy to chop up fruits and nuts for breakfast and to make massive salads for lunch. For dinner, I would be exhausted from the hour-long drive home, and I would make quick stir-fries and sautés.

My switch to eating a lot more colorful fruits and veggies inspired me to create and experiment more. So, here we are a few years later, with my blog *Vegan Yack Attack*, my first cookbook, *Vegan Bowl Attack!*, and now this. My mission with this book is to give you a wide variety of meals that are fun, tasty, and quick to put together. On the flip side, I have some chapters that will help you literally eat *on the go*! The recipes are portable and can be prepped ahead, or you can keep them on hand while you're traveling to make your life easier. It is fun getting back to my cooking roots and continuing to make eating vegan more fun—and incredibly delicious— for everyone.

CHAPTER 1

VEGAN EATING MADE EASY

More often than not, the idea of switching around your food life can be daunting. The pantry, methods, and tools you are familiar with may not be the same as those you use with vegan cooking. Have no fear, I will cover the basics for you to make this as painless as possible. While some ingredients may be a little peculiar, 95 percent of them are usually quite easy to find.

PANTRY NECESSITIES

Let's talk about what foods you will be needing for this book—and awesome vegan cooking in general.

BEANS/LEGUMES

These will be your allergy-friendly source of protein, fiber, and a variety of minerals. Having both dried and cooked/canned beans on hand is always a good idea! Black beans, white beans, kidney beans, chickpeas, the possibilities are nearly endless—and very affordable. Lentils are some of my favorite legumes, and the red ones cook up quickly!

NUTS AND SEEDS

I love always having jars of different nuts and seeds on deck. Roasted or raw, shelled or not, most nuts and seeds can easily be found in grocery stores, or even big-box stores for a better deal. Both foods contain varying levels of healthy fats and protein, and are a great topping for all kinds of meals. Using nut and seed butters is another way to get these nutrients into your meals, especially with options such as almond, sunflower, and peanut butter.

TOFU AND TEMPEH

If you do not have a soy allergy, both of these foods are great options for a filling, low-fat source of protein. They are highly adaptable, soaking up anything you marinate them in, and they can be used in so many dishes, both savory and sweet. The difference between the two is that tofu is made from curdled soymilk, while tempeh is a patty of fermented soybeans. You can find them at most grocery stores, health food stores, and Asian markets.

SEITAN AND VITAL WHEAT GLUTEN

In the case of seitan, a high-protein wheat meat, if you do not have a gluten allergy it is a great way to bulk up your meals. It is made of vital wheat gluten, the protein of wheat, and liquids and seasonings combined to create a stretchy, chewy meat substitute. Homemade seitan is versatile in the way that it can be used in place of deli slices, chicken breast, sausages, and more. For convenience, you can also find premade seitan products in most health food stores and some grocery stores.

RICE AND GRAINS

When I wrote my first cookbook, I got even more familiar with the rice and grain family than I was before! Rice is great for providing energy because it is high in carbohydrates and low in fat, and can stabilize blood sugar levels. There are many different kinds, but I think that brown and white are easiest to find. Grains like wild rice, quinoa, buckwheat, farro, and oats all have different benefits and are a solid accompaniment to any dish.

NUTRITIONAL YEAST

This vegan staple gets its own mention because it is awesome! It is also a really confusing product to those who may be new to vegan cooking. Nutritional yeast is an inactive yeast that is yellow, and it has a savory, nutty, and slightly cheesy flavor. Vegan cheese sauces, soups, and other savory creations are given an extra oomph when made with this ingredient. You can find it in the bulk, supplement, or spice sections of most health food stores.

OILS

I like to keep a variety of oils on hand. There is a popular misconception that one oil will work for all things. Do you need a million? No. But you should have one oil for high-heat cooking, roasting, and sautéing, such as sunflower, avocado, or coconut oil. Olive oil and sesame oil are both good finishing oils for stirring in at the end of a recipe, making vinaigrettes, or drizzling on top. Refined coconut oil is also a good stand-in for butter when baking because it is firm and has no coconut flavor. Having a high-heat cooking oil spray is also good for roasting and sautéing if you want to use less oil.

VINEGARS

These acidic liquids balance out flavors in a multitude of ways. The mainstays in my pantry are raw apple cider, white, rice, and balsamic vinegars. Those vinegars will cover a large array of recipes and are easily found, but there are some others that have special purposes. I love using coconut vinegar in vegan cheese sauces because it is not as sweet as apple cider vinegar, yet gives it the sharpness of fermented cheese. I also use red wine vinegar for dressings, stir-fries, and occasionally soups.

FLOURS AND STARCHES

I'm really into baking, so I always have a few types of flours on hand. Unbleached all-purpose flour, whole wheat pastry flour, and a gluten-free flour blend will cover almost any need! Two special flours that are also good to have are brown rice flour and chickpea flour. Brown rice flour gets really crunchy, so it's perfect in crusted or breaded recipes, while chickpea flour is high in protein and can be used to make egg-like dishes. Arrowroot, corn, and tapioca starches can mostly be used interchangeably, but they are not exactly the same. All of these foods can be easily found in most grocery stores.

PASTA, BREAD, AND TORTILLAS

These carb-y items are essential for making quick meals. The only thing you need to worry about is checking the ingredients list! Pasta can sometimes contain egg; bread can have dairy, eggs, or honey; tortillas may contain lard or even milk powder. There are helpful apps that can save you time by looking up strange ingredients to see if they are vegan, which makes shopping less stressful.

NONDAIRY MILKS

There are many options for those looking to omit dairy from their diet. The most popular nondairy milk right now, without a doubt, is almond milk. Soy, hemp, coconut, cashew, rice, oat, and even pea milks are also all over the place! I typically buy the unsweetened, plain varieties, so that I can use them in any recipe and control the amount of sweetness easily. For multipurpose, I reach for the almond milk. For heavy cream recipes, such as ice cream or whipped cream, canned, full-fat coconut milk is perfect.

HERBS AND SPICES

Nothing is sadder than a pantry absent of dried herbs and spices. These are some of the most affordable ways that you can make a tasty dish without a large variety of fresh ingredients on hand. With herbs and spices, you can take a potato and make it a comforting, garlicky mash, or go with a spicy Cajun hash instead.

VEGAN SPECIALTY PRODUCTS

Making everything from scratch all of the time can be so rewarding! It can also seem like a huge hassle. So, for those times when you need a shortcut, you can buy vegan versions of all your standard fare. Typically, I always have vegan mayo, cheese shreds or slices, sour cream, and a few sauces on hand. Sometimes using that store-bought teriyaki saves 10 minutes off of a 30 minute-meal! As mentioned before, seitan or vegan meats are fairly accessible now. Use them when you aren't feeling up to making your own.

FRUITS AND VEGETABLES

Last, but most important, you will need fruits and vegetables to really nail this vegan cooking thing. Buying produce that is organic and in season is important to me, but I know it is not always realistic. Even keeping dried fruits and frozen veggies in the freezer can keep you prepared for a healthy breakfast or weeknight dinner. This is especially true when you leave town and come back to an empty fridge. I cannot stress enough that you should try and be open to new ingredients. Before I went vegan I did not eat half of the foods I eat now. Believe me, I'm much better off for it!

EQUIPMENT

This category is pretty straightforward if you have a general idea of how to cook. But, having experienced my cousin's home after she just moved in, I know some people are starting from literally nothing! Hopefully, this list can help you stock your kitchen for a lifetime of awesome meals.

SHARP KNIFE AND CUTTING BOARD

With these two tools, you will get far! You don't need to spend an arm and a leg on a quality knife. My favorite knife—that I've used for six years and also have a tattoo of—is my Shun Santoku knife. I'm not joking when I say that I use this knife for 98 percent of my cutting. Finding a similar blade or chef's knife is easy, and as long as you keep it sharp, it'll be safer and more efficient. Of course, you'll want to have a cutting board. I prefer wood and bamboo because they're easier on your blade, but plastic ones will also work.

MIXING BOWLS

Having three or four mixing bowls of different sizes is always a good idea. Plus, they can double as serving dishes if you lack storage space.

MEASURING SPOONS AND CUPS

If you want to follow a recipe, you will definitely need these! I have two sets of measuring spoons, one set of dry measuring cups, and a couple liquid measuring cups.

UTENSILS

As basics, it is helpful to have at least one each of these: whisk, silicone spatula, slotted spoon, wooden spoon, grater, citrus reamer, can opener, ladle, kitchen shears, ice cream scoop, vegetable peeler, sifter, tongs, rolling pin, and obviously, eating utensils. I also have some specialty tools such as a microplane for zesting, a pastry brush for applying oil or even BBQ sauce, and a garlic press. A good way to select kitchen tools is to ask, can this be used for multiple purposes? For example, you can use an ice cream scoop to scoop ice cream, and it will also effortlessly fill cupcake liners with batter.

SCALE

For the longest time, I didn't own a scale. After getting one for my first cookbook, I've been kicking myself for not investing sooner. Scales help weigh ingredients for the most accurate measurement, and that can be helpful for sliced or chopped ingredients. A scale is especially useful for baking because measurements need to be precise.

PANS, POTS, AND SKILLETS

When I think of cooking, these are the items that immediately come to mind. For me, the bare minimum is at least one sauté pan, one pot, and a cast-iron skillet. You can find affordable cookware sets at most home goods stores.

BLENDER

One of my most-used appliances is my blender. I use it for puréeing smoothies, soups, and sauces; grinding flours; making powdered sugar in a pinch; and so much more. Of course, some blenders are better than others, so if you're just getting into cooking, don't feel like you need to start with an expensive, high-speed blender. But, if you find yourself blending often, it is a worthy investment.

FOOD PROCESSOR

Though the blender and this appliance have some overlapping capabilities, I use my food processor all the time. I find it better for coarse grinds and for making crusts, pesto, nut butters, veggie burgers, and even ice cream. An added bonus is that you can buy different discs for your processor (some come with it) to grate, slice, and mix, quickly and easily.

BAKING SHEETS AND DISHES

Baking sheets set you up to roast or toast ingredients, bake cookies, or even make chips. Start out with at least one large baking sheet and one small sheet. Baking dishes, on the other hand, are great for casseroles, enchiladas, brownies, or whatever you put your mind to! You should have one large rectangular dish and one square dish to start out. Cupcake pans, cake pans, and cooling racks can be lumped in here as well; they are great for baking and non-baking purposes.

PARCHMENT PAPER, FOIL, AND SILICONE MATS

Some of these items are interchangeable, but I think all are essential. Parchment paper is great for baking and for preventing you from making a huge mess. Foil can be used to hold food for cooking or grilling. Foil is also great for covering food while baking, or lining baking sheets for an extra-crispy roast. The silicone mat is an easy-to-clean, eco-friendly, nonstick way to bake and roast food in the oven; mine has been through a lot and is still holding strong.

COOKERS

For the recipes in this book, a pressure cooker, slow cooker, or Instant Pot will come in handy. Do you need one of each? No, but I've found that it helps immensely with bulk cooking. The Instant Pot is a bit of a game-changer because it can slow cook, pressure cook, sauté, and more. So, if you do not have a ton of kitchen space, this multiuse cooker is perfect.

SMALL APPLIANCES

Some of these are not necessary, but are extremely useful and can be used in various applications. An electric coffee grinder is great for grinding coffee, of course, but also for grinding spices, seeds, and even dried fruit. Another small appliance that I love is the immersion blender; it is good for blending soups in the pot, making vegan mayo, and emulsifying in general.

FOOD STORAGE CONTAINERS

Reusable food containers are priceless for the home cook, especially for this book! Find containers that are of various sizes, and made of either glass, stainless steel, or BPA-free plastic. I end up using a lot of glass jars because they are affordable, easy to store, and great for canning and preserving.

HELPFUL TIPS AND TRICKS

I have learned so much about cooking vegan food over the years, and I continue to do so. Here are just some of the many tips I can give you that will help you get started.

TREAT YOUR REFRIGERATOR LIKE A SALAD BAR.

Keeping a handful of items at the ready in your refrigerator will make eating vegan on the go a breeze. Chop up some of your favorite veggies—such as carrots, broccoli, kale, and onions—and store them in separate containers. Cook a large batch of lentils or chickpeas for the week to add them to any dish for a boost of protein and fiber. My friend Michelle keeps a jar of chia seeds soaked in water in her fridge to add to smoothies, oats, and other dishes. Soaked chia seeds will keep for up to a week.

ADD CREAMINESS TO ANY DISH.

You wouldn't think it with vegan being dairy-free, but there are plenty of ways to add a creamy element to dishes. Some of my favorites are soaked-and-blended cashews, steamed-and-puréed cauliflower, silken tofu, puréed white beans, and coconut milk.

EASILY COOK OIL FREE.

Most dishes can be made oil-free without too much of a headache! Instead of sautéing with oil, use a thin layer of vegetable broth. For baking, you can usually substitute puréed banana, apples, or even pumpkin for oil. The end result is not exactly the same, but it's still delicious.

REPLACE EGGS.

There are a bevy of choices when it comes to replacing eggs, but they all have specific uses. You can use applesauce and mashed banana in place of eggs when baking breads, cakes, and the like. Aquafaba, a.k.a. chickpea brine, has wowed everyone with its ability to make vegan meringues, marshmallow crème, mayo, and so much more. Ground flaxseed or chia seeds can be whisked together with warm water to create a gelatinous egg for baking.

GET YOUR VEGGIES IN.

Sometimes I make a recipe and it's pretty amazing, but I'm not sure there are enough vegetables included. Before plating, grab a handful of salad greens and make a bed for your dish to sit on. Now, you have an extra cup of greens, effortlessly. This is the reason I love getting the big salad green containers from the store.

TRY THIS RAPID-FIRE COOKING ADVICE.

When chopping your veggies, keep the pieces the same size so that they cook evenly. Always keep your pan handles over the stove when cooking; you don't want to knock them off! Wear glasses while chopping onions to help avoid tears. Taste and season your food as you go. Never be afraid to experiment, and possibly fail—that's how you learn!

RECIPE GUIDES

Beneath each recipe title there are helpful guides to let you know how quick and easy, portable, or allergy-friendly a recipe may be. Here is a little elaboration on each one, so that you know what you're getting into.

UNDER 10 INGREDIENTS
This recipe will use 10 ingredients or less, not counting salt, pepper, or water.

30 MINUTES OR LESS
This recipe will take 30 minutes or less to cook.

PORTABLE
You can make this recipe ahead of time, and it travels well.

MAKE-AHEAD
This recipe can be made ahead of time, but it may not travel well.

ONE-PAN
This recipe can be made using one pot, pan, or baking sheet.

GLUTEN FREE
This recipe does not include any gluten.

SOY FREE
This recipe is free of any and all soy products.

NUT FREE
This recipe does not contain any form of nut.

OIL FREE
There is no oil added to this recipe, though there may be ingredients containing low amounts of oil.

SUGAR FREE
This recipe does not contain added sugars such as white sugar, turbinado sugar, maple syrup, agave nectar, or other refined varieties. It may contain coconut sugar.

CHAPTER 2

QUICK BREAKFASTS, SNACKS, AND TREATS

GET THROUGH THE DAY WITH SOME PEP IN YOUR STEP

Would you rather sleep a little longer in the morning or enjoy a decent breakfast before rushing to work? Now you can have both! Here are some tasty breakfasts to start your day, plus some little desserts for the perfect ending.

CHEEZY CHICKPEA SCRAMBLE

• UNDER 10 INGREDIENTS • 30 MINUTES OR LESS • ONE PAN
• GLUTEN FREE • SOY FREE • NUT FREE • SUGAR FREE

Tofu scrambles are easy and filling, but sometimes you need a soy-free version to help accommodate everyone! This chickpea scramble still has some eggy flavor from the Indian black salt (kala namak), and it is really great on a piece of toast.

1 tablespoon (15 ml) sunflower oil

1 cup (140 g) diced yellow onion

2 cans (30 ounces, or 850 g) chickpeas, drained, liquid (a.k.a. aquafaba) reserved

2 teaspoons (3 g) cornstarch

⅓ cup (25 g) nutritional yeast

1 teaspoon Indian black salt (kala namak), or more to taste

¼ teaspoon black pepper, or more to taste

2 cups (80 g) chopped kale, loosely packed with stems removed

2 cups (180 g) sliced button mushrooms

1 cup (185 g) chopped tomatoes

Warm the sunflower oil in a large skillet over medium heat. Once a drop of water sizzles on the skillet, add the yellow onions and chickpeas. Sauté 3 to 5 minutes, or until the onions are translucent. In a small bowl, whisk ¼ cup (60 ml) aquafaba and cornstarch together until combined and frothy.

Add the aquafaba mixture to the skillet and cook until it thickens, about 2 to 3 minutes. Add the nutritional yeast, Indian black salt, and pepper, stirring until coated. Add the kale, button mushrooms, and tomatoes, sautéing until the kale has wilted and the mushrooms have softened and reduced in size.

Season with more Indian black salt and pepper, if needed, to taste. Serve warm.

YIELD: 4 SERVINGS

NOTE: INDIAN BLACK SALT IS A SULFUR-RICH SALT THAT COMES FROM INDIA, AND IT IS USED TO IMPART AN EGGY FLAVOR TO DISHES THAT ARE EGG-FREE! DESPITE ITS NAME, BLACK SALT HAS MORE OF A ROSE COLOR WHEN GROUND DOWN. IT CAN BE FOUND IN INDIAN MARKETS, SOME NATURAL FOOD STORES, OR ONLINE.

CREAMY BERRY-FULL POLENTA

- UNDER 10 INGREDIENTS • 30 MINUTES OR LESS
- GLUTEN FREE • SOY FREE • NUT-FREE OPTION • OIL FREE

Are you sick of oats? I don't think I'll ever be, but it is still nice to switch up my grains in the morning. Polenta cooked with non-dairy milk is extra creamy and goes wonderfully with warmed berries. Extra points for keeping some Simple Cashew Cream (page 186) on hand to dollop onto this delicious breakfast.

2 cups (470 ml) unsweetened nondairy milk

1 cup (235 ml) water

1 cup (140 g) polenta grits

¼ cup (60 ml) maple syrup

Pinch of salt

FOR THE TOPPING:

1 cup (145 g) fresh blueberries

1 cup (140 g) fresh blackberries

2 tablespoons (30 ml) water

¼ cup (60 ml) Simple Cashew Cream
   (page 186; optional)

In a large pot over medium-high heat, bring the nondairy milk and water to a boil. Stir in the polenta grits, and adjust the heat to medium-low. Cook—covered but vented, stirring occasionally—for 18 to 20 minutes, or until the polenta is creamy. Stir in the maple syrup, and add salt to taste. Keep warm until ready to serve.

While the polenta is cooking, warm the blueberries, blackberries, and water in a small saucepan over medium heat. Bring to a simmer, adjust the heat to medium-low, and cook until the berries start to break down, about 10 minutes. Lightly mash the berries if they are not breaking apart.

Divide the creamy polenta between 4 bowls, and top each with some berry mixture. Dollop 1 tablespoon (15 ml) of Simple Cashew Cream on top of each bowl (if using), and serve warm.

YIELD: 4 SERVINGS

NOTE: IF YOU DO NOT HAVE FRESH BERRIES ON HAND, FROZEN WILL ALSO WORK. YOU MAY HAVE TO COOK THEM LONGER BECAUSE THEY RETAIN MORE WATER.

RECOVERY SMOOTHIE

Believe it or not, this recipe first originated from the need to recover from a hangover. Oops. But I've found that it is also great for recovering from intense workouts, or even working all-nighters.

2 cups (400 g) sliced frozen bananas
4 pitted dates (65 g)
3 tablespoons (30 g) cocoa powder
2 tablespoons (23 g) hemp seeds
½ teaspoon ground cinnamon
Pinch of salt
1 cup (235 ml) coconut water
Ice (optional)

Place all ingredients in a blender and purée until completely smooth. Add ice while blending, if you would like a colder smoothie. Serve.

YIELD: 2 SERVINGS

TIP: IF YOUR DATES SEEM TOUGH OR DRY, SOAK THEM IN HOT WATER FOR 10 MINUTES, THEN DRAIN. THIS SHOULD GIVE YOUR BLENDER A BIT OF A BREAK!

FRESH FRUIT YOGURT SUNDAE

• UNDER 10 INGREDIENTS • 30 MINUTES OR LESS • PORTABLE

• GLUTEN FREE • SOY FREE • OIL FREE

Sometimes I just want a sweet treat for breakfast. This yogurt sundae fits the bill perfectly because it has rich chocolate, combines sweet and salty flavors, and comes together in under 10 minutes. Customize the fruit to the season you are in for tasty variations.

6 tablespoons (65 g) vegan chocolate chips

2 tablespoons (30 ml) unsweetened nondairy milk

3 cups (705 ml) plain nondairy yogurt

2 cups (280 g) sliced banana

2 cups (300 g) quartered strawberries

1 cup (175 g) halved grapes

¼ cup (40 g) roasted, salted peanuts

1 tablespoon (15 ml) maple syrup (optional)

In a small mixing bowl, combine the chocolate chips and nondairy milk. Microwave for 45 seconds. Whisk together until combined and smooth.

Divide the yogurt between 4 bowls, along with the fresh fruit and peanuts. Drizzle chocolate sauce over the top and add maple syrup if you prefer your yogurt sweeter.

YIELD: 4 SERVINGS

TIP: TO MAKE THIS MORE DESSERT-LIKE, USE VANILLA OR A FRUITY NONDAIRY YOGURT INSTEAD OF PLAIN.

BLUEBERRY ZUCCHINI BREAKFAST COOKIES

• PORTABLE • MAKE AHEAD
• GLUTEN-FREE OPTION • SOY FREE

Sometimes when I wake up after not enough sleep, the thought of making even a smoothie can seem like too much work. Yes, I am that lazy. That's why I love baking these delicious breakfast cookies when I'm up for it and saving them to eat throughout the week!

1½ cups (120 g) rolled oats, gluten free if necessary

1 cup (130 g) unbleached all-purpose flour, or gluten-free flour with ½ teaspoon xanthan gum

½ teaspoon baking powder

½ teaspoon baking soda

¼ teaspoon salt

½ cup (115 ml) orange juice

½ cup (72 g) coconut sugar

½ cup (60 g) shredded zucchini

¼ cup (60 ml) melted coconut oil

1 tablespoon (5 g) ground flaxseed

2 teaspoons (10 ml) vanilla extract

2 teaspoons (4 g) orange zest

1 teaspoon molasses

½ cup (75 g) blueberries

½ cup (100 g) chopped pecans

Preheat the oven to 350°F (180°C, or gas mark 4), and line two large baking sheets with parchment paper.

In a large mixing bowl, whisk together the oats, flour, baking powder, baking soda, and salt. In a medium mixing bowl, whisk together the orange juice, coconut sugar, zucchini, coconut oil, flaxseed, vanilla, orange zest, and molasses until combined.

Create a well in the dry ingredients, then pour the wet ingredients into it. Fold the dough together until there are no dry spots in the mixture. Add the blueberries and pecans to the dough, and fold together until incorporated evenly.

Place ¼-cup-sized (roughly 90 g) scoops, 2 inches (5 cm) apart on the baking sheets. Press down gently to flatten the cookies slightly. Bake for 20 to 24 minutes, switching the baking sheet positions halfway through. When the cookies are done baking they will be soft—leave the sheets on cooling racks for 15 to 20 minutes before serving them.

YIELD: 12 COOKIES

CRUSTLESS QUICHE BITES

• PORTABLE • MAKE AHEAD
• GLUTEN FREE • SOY FREE • NUT FREE • SUGAR FREE

My mom made some amazing quiche while I was growing up, and though we mostly ate it for dinner I love the idea of these Crustless Quiche Bites being a tasty addition to any breakfast. Eat a couple of these with a banana and some greens, and you have a satiating, delicious first meal.

Cooking oil spray

1 tablespoon (15 ml) sunflower oil

1 cup (85 g) chopped broccoli florets

1 cup (40 g) baby spinach

¼ cup (40 g) diced red onion

⅓ cup (50 g) diced sun-dried tomatoes

1¼ cups (155 g) chickpea flour

⅓ cup (25 g) nutritional yeast

1½ tablespoons (12 g) cornstarch

2 teaspoons Indian black salt (kala namak, see note on page 21)

1 teaspoon onion powder

¼ teaspoon ground turmeric

¼ teaspoon black pepper

2¼ cups (530 ml) vegetable broth

1 teaspoon apple cider vinegar

Preheat the oven to 350°F (180°C, or gas mark 4), and spray a 12-count cupcake pan with a thin coat of cooking oil spray.

Warm the sunflower oil in a small sauté pan over medium heat. Once a drop of water sizzles on the pan, add the broccoli, spinach, red onions, and sun-dried tomatoes. Sauté for 5 minutes, or until the onions become nearly translucent. Set the pan aside while you mix the batter.

In a large mixing bowl, whisk the chickpea flour, nutritional yeast, cornstarch, Indian black salt, onion powder, turmeric, and black pepper together until evenly combined.

Add the vegetable broth and apple cider vinegar to the chickpea flour mixture, whisking until combined. Fold the sautéed mixture into the batter and ladle roughly ⅓ cup (80 ml) of it into each opening in the cupcake pan. Bake for 25 to 28 minutes, or until the tops are golden and are not too jiggly when you bump the pan.

Cool the pan on a rack for 10 minutes before serving the quiche bites.

YIELD: 12 QUICHE BITES

TIP: IF YOU'D LIKE TO FREEZE THESE QUICHE BITES FOR LATER, LET THEM COOL DOWN FULLY BEFORE PLACING IN A ZIP BAG. WHEN REHEATING, ALLOW THE QUICHE BITES TO DEFROST FIRST, THEN WARM THEM IN THE MICROWAVE OR OVEN.

LOADED AVOCADO LENTIL TOAST

- UNDER 10 INGREDIENTS - 30 MINUTES OR LESS
- GLUTEN-FREE OPTION - SOY FREE - NUT FREE - SUGAR FREE

I think we all know that avocado toast has become the staple snack in houses worldwide, but I wanted to do my own, well-rounded take on this simple breakfast. Lentils provide the protein and added fiber, tomatoes pair incredibly well with buttery avocado, and fresh herbs bring some amazing flavors.

4 slices thick-cut bread, gluten-free if necessary

Cooking oil spray

1 large avocado (200 g)

1 cup (285 g) cooked green or black lentils

½ cup (150 g) sliced tomatoes

1 tablespoon (3 g) minced cilantro or basil

¼ teaspoon coarse salt

⅛ teaspoon black pepper

Coat the 4 slices of bread lightly with cooking oil spray and toast them until golden brown. Slice the avocado and divide it among the bread slices, spreading it out evenly. Top each with ¼ cup (70 g) of lentils, a couple of slices of tomato, minced herbs, salt, and pepper. Serve warm.

YIELD: 4 SERVINGS

NOTE: SOME GROCERY STORES SELL COOKED LENTILS IN THEIR REFRIGERATED AREA, OR THEY SELL CANNED COOKED LENTILS. AS NOTED IN THE FIRST CHAPTER (PAGE 16), YOU CAN BULK COOK LENTILS TO HAVE READY IN YOUR REFRIGERATOR FOR RECIPES LIKE THIS!

FROZEN PINEAPPLE FLOATS

• 30 MINUTES OR LESS • UNDER 10 INGREDIENTS
• GLUTEN FREE • SOY FREE • NUT FREE • OIL FREE • SUGAR-FREE OPTION

So, these Frozen Pineapple Floats were inspired by one of my favorite treats to get while at Disneyland. It seems so simple, but the creamy soft serve paired with chilled pineapple juice is ultra-refreshing.

3 cups (395 g) frozen pineapple chunks

⅔ cup (190 g) thick cream from full-fat coconut milk

1 tablespoon (15 ml) agave nectar (optional)

4 cups (940 ml) pineapple juice

4 cherries, for garnish (optional)

Place the frozen pineapple and coconut cream in a food processor, processing with an S-blade until very smooth. Add agave if you would like a sweeter soft serve, and process again until combined.

Freeze the mixture for 15 minutes, then scoop the soft serve into 4 glasses. Pour 1 cup (235 ml) of pineapple juice into each glass and garnish with a cherry (if using). Serve immediately.

YIELD: 4 SERVINGS

TIP: THESE FLOATS LOOK DARLING WITH SOME FANCY UMBRELLAS STUCK THROUGH THE CHERRY GARNISH!

BEASTLY CAULIFLOWER BREAKFAST BURRITO

• PORTABLE • MAKE AHEAD
• GLUTEN-FREE OPTION • SOY FREE • NUT FREE

Ever since I was on my high school surf team—yes, that was a thing—breakfast burritos have been a staple in my diet. Filling, make-ahead, and delicious, this beast is filled with an old favorite (potatoes) and some new twists on classics with the cauliflower scramble and maple pinto sausage!

FOR THE BREAKFAST POTATOES:

1½ tablespoons (25 ml) sunflower oil

1 pound (453 g) russet potatoes, chopped

1 cup (145 g) diced green bell pepper

1 cup (140 g) diced white onion

¼ cup (60 ml) water

½ teaspoon salt, or to taste

⅛ teaspoon pepper, or to taste

FOR THE CAULIFLOWER SCRAMBLE:

1 teaspoon sunflower oil

1½ pounds (685 g) cauliflower florets, chopped

¼ cup (20 g) nutritional yeast

1 teaspoon Indian black salt
   (kala namak; see note page 21)

1 teaspoon onion powder

¼ teaspoon black pepper

¼ teaspoon ground turmeric

FOR THE MAPLE PINTO SAUSAGE:

1 teaspoon sunflower oil

1 can (15 ounces, or 425 g) pinto beans,
   drained and rinsed

1½ teaspoons maple syrup

½ teaspoon fennel seed

½ teaspoon dried sage

½ teaspoon smoked paprika

¼ to ½ teaspoon salt

⅛ teaspoon black pepper

FOR THE ASSEMBLY:

4 large flour or gluten-free tortillas

½ cup (120 g) salsa

TO MAKE THE BREAKFAST POTATOES:

Warm the sunflower oil in a large skillet over medium-high heat. Once hot, add the potatoes, stirring occasionally, until the potatoes are golden brown—roughly 10 minutes. Add the bell peppers and white onions, sautéing for 5 more minutes.

Reduce the heat to medium-low, add water to the skillet, and cover with a lid, simmering for 5 minutes, or until the potatoes are fork tender. Keep warm, uncovered, on low heat, adding salt and pepper, to taste.

TO MAKE THE CAULIFLOWER SCRAMBLE:

Warm the sunflower oil in a large sauté pan over medium heat. Add the cauliflower to the pan, sautéing for 5 to 7 minutes, or until it has softened and reduced in size. Stir in the nutritional yeast, Indian black salt, onion powder, black pepper, and turmeric until the cauliflower is evenly coated. Keep warm on low heat.

TO MAKE THE MAPLE PINTO SAUSAGE:

Warm the sunflower oil in a small sauté pan over medium heat. Add the pinto beans to the pan, and cook until heated through, stirring occasionally. Stir in the maple syrup, fennel seed, sage, smoked paprika, salt, and black pepper, cooking for another 3 minutes.

TO ASSEMBLE:

Microwave the tortillas for 30 seconds to soften them and make them more pliable. Divide the breakfast potatoes, cauliflower scramble, and maple pinto sausage between the 4 tortillas, then top each with salsa. Fold two sides of the tortilla toward the middle, then roll the end closest to you over the filling. Keep rolling until the burrito is completely closed. Serve warm, or wrap in foil to freeze for later!

YIELD: 4 BURRITOS

TIP: IT MAY ADD A COUPLE OF EXTRA MINUTES TO THIS RECIPE, BUT TOASTING THE BURRITOS IN A LARGE PAN OVER MEDIUM HEAT FOR 2 TO 3 MINUTES ON TWO SIDES IS A BURRITO GAME-CHANGER, AND I HIGHLY RECOMMEND IT!

CHOCOLATE CHERRY CUPS

• UNDER 10 INGREDIENTS • PORTABLE • MAKE AHEAD
• GLUTEN FREE • SOY FREE

While the combination of peanut butter and chocolate is probably one of my favorites, dark sweet cherries covered in chocolate comes pretty close to touching it. These cups come together easily, and the result feels so indulgent!

½ cup (120 ml) melted coconut oil
⅓ cup (25 g) cocoa powder
½ cup (120 ml) agave nectar
18 dark sweet cherries, pitted
¼ cup (35 g) toasted cashews, finely chopped
¼ teaspoon coarse salt

In a 24-count mini-cupcake pan, place 18 mini-cupcake liners. In a mixing bowl, whisk together the coconut oil, cocoa powder, and agave nectar until very smooth. Spoon 1 teaspoon of the chocolate mixture into each of the 18 mini-cupcake liners.

Gently set a pitted cherry into each cup, topping with roughly 1½ teaspoons chocolate mixture, followed by toasted cashews and coarse salt. Freeze for 35 to 40 minutes to set. Store these cups in the refrigerator.

YIELD: 18 CUPS

TIP: IF YOU HAVE A METAL DRINKING STRAW IN YOUR KITCHEN, USE IT TO PIT FRESH CHERRIES BY POKING THE STEM THROUGH THE OPENING OF THE STRAW, THEN PUSHING THROUGH THE CHERRY—WATCH YOUR FINGERS—AND OUT THE OTHER SIDE. BOOM! PIT REMOVED.

GREEN PEACH SMOOTHIE

● UNDER 10 INGREDIENTS ● 30 MINUTES OR LESS ● PORTABLE
● GLUTEN FREE ● SOY FREE ● NUT FREE ● OIL FREE ● SUGAR FREE

Can you really have a vegan cookbook without a green smoothie recipe? I mean, yes, but I thought I'd include one of my new favorite smoothie combinations with a sneaky ingredient: zucchini! If you don't care for bananas in your smoothies, zucchini is a great substitute, as its flavor is fairly neutral.

1 cup (125 g) chopped zucchini

1 cup (45 g) baby spinach, packed

2½ cups (345 g) chopped frozen peaches

1 cup (235 ml) unsweetened nondairy milk

½ teaspoon ground ginger, or more to taste

¼ teaspoon ground turmeric, or more to taste

Place all the ingredients in a blender in the order listed. Blend until completely smooth. Taste the smoothie mixture, adding more ginger or turmeric, to taste.

Divide the smoothie between 2 glasses, and serve.

YIELD: 2 SERVINGS

NOTE: WHEN PEACHES ARE OUT OF SEASON, TRY SWITCHING THEM WITH FROZEN STRAWBERRIES OR APPLES.

LEMON LAVENDER MINI CHEESECAKES

• PORTABLE • MAKE AHEAD
• GLUTEN FREE • SOY FREE

For a long time, I thought I hated all flower flavors in food. Turns out, it's just rose! So, here we have subtly sweet, mostly raw mini cheesecakes with calming lavender and tart lemon. They're inspired by mini cheesecakes my parents used to have on hand always, in case we had guests. Or if my dad got a hankering for sweets.

FOR THE FILLING:

1½ cups (205 g) raw cashews

¾ cup (175 ml) water

¼ cup (60 ml) maple syrup or agave nectar

1 tablespoon (15 ml) lemon juice

1 tablespoon (15 ml) coconut oil

1½ teaspoons vanilla extract

1 teaspoon fresh lavender

1 teaspoon lemon zest

¼ teaspoon salt

FOR THE CRUST:

1 cup (105 g) walnuts

½ cup (100 g) dates, pitted

⅛ teaspoon salt

TO ASSEMBLE:

48 small lavender leaves

6 thin lemon slices, quartered

TO MAKE THE FILLING:

Place the raw cashews, water, maple syrup, lemon juice, coconut oil, vanilla, lavender, lemon zest, and salt in a blender. Purée until mostly smooth, then allow the cashews to soak up some of the liquid for 5 to 7 minutes (while waiting, make the crust). Blend again until very smooth.

TO MAKE THE CRUST:

In a food processor, place the walnuts, dates, and salt. Pulse until the mixture resembles large grains of sand, and will stick together when pinched. Line a mini-cupcake pan with 24 mini-cupcake liners, then press roughly 1½ teaspoons of the crust mixture into the bottom of each one.

TO ASSEMBLE:

Pour roughly 4 teaspoons (20 ml) of cheesecake mixture into each cup, then gently top with 2 lavender leaves and 1 piece of lemon. Freeze for at least 1 hour to set.

YIELD: 24 CHEESECAKE BITES

NOTE: I STORE THESE CHEESECAKE BITES IN MY FREEZER SO THAT I CAN PULL ONE OUT AS A MINI-DESSERT WHENEVER I HAVE A CRAVING. THEY ONLY TAKE 4 TO 6 MINUTES TO SOFTEN ENOUGH FOR A QUICK SNACK!

NO-BAKE APRICOT ALMOND BARS

• UNDER 10 INGREDIENTS • 30 MINUTES OR LESS • PORTABLE • MAKE AHEAD
• GLUTEN FREE • SOY FREE • OIL FREE

While I love eating dried fruits for energy, adding nuts and seeds to the mix creates a more nutritionally well-rounded snack. When you put them all together with a sweet yogurt drizzle, you get these quick and easy no-bake bars, which are perfect for hiking, post-workout eats, or just getting rid of hunger between meals.

FOR THE BARS:

1½ cups (240 g) dried apricots

1½ cups (210 g) raw almonds

½ cup (70 g) raw sunflower seeds

2 tablespoons (30 ml) maple syrup

⅛ teaspoon salt

FOR THE DRIZZLE:

¼ cup (45 g) vegan white chocolate chips

2 tablespoons (30 g) plain nondairy yogurt

TO MAKE THE BARS:

Place the apricots, almonds, sunflower seeds, maple syrup, and salt in a food processor. Process with an S-blade until the mixture resembles large grains of sand, and will stick together when pinched.

Press the bar mixture into the bottom of an 8-inch (20.5 cm) square or 6 x 10-inch (15 x 25 cm) baking dish lined with parchment paper, and set aside.

TO MAKE THE DRIZZLE:

Place the white chocolate chips in a microwave-safe bowl. Microwave them for 45 to 60 seconds, or until they are melted. Add the yogurt to the bowl and whisk together until smooth, then drizzle over the bars.

Refrigerate the baking dish for 15 minutes to allow the drizzle to set. Then slice into 8 equal bars, which you can wrap separately in wax or parchment paper for snacking later, or serve immediately. Store these bars in the refrigerator when not serving.

YIELD: 8 BARS

PUMPKIN MAPLE DONUT HOLES

• 30 MINUTES OR LESS • PORTABLE • MAKE AHEAD
• GLUTEN FREE • OIL FREE

You know, when I started on these "donut holes" it was something different. I was going to go for some truffles, but a few mistakes and then finessing later, I came out of the other side with a snack that you won't be able to resist. They reminded me of the crumb donuts I used to eat as a child, hence the name! And I won't tell others they're healthy if you don't.

FOR THE DONUT HOLES:

1½ cups (225 g) roasted almonds

¾ cup (180 g) pumpkin purée

⅓ cup (80 ml) maple syrup

½ teaspoon ground cinnamon

¼ teaspoon ground ginger

¼ teaspoon salt

⅛ teaspoon ground cloves

⅛ teaspoon ground nutmeg

¼ cup (40 g) chia seeds

1 cup (100 g) loosely packed gluten-free or vegan graham cracker crumbs, divided

FOR THE CREAM CHEESE DIPPING SAUCE:

¼ cup (60 g) vegan cream cheese

2 tablespoons (30 ml) maple syrup

TO MAKE THE DONUT HOLES:

Place the almonds in a food processor and process with an S-blade for 5 minutes, or until they have nearly turned to almond butter. Add the pumpkin, maple syrup, cinnamon, ginger, salt, cloves, and nutmeg to the almonds, pulsing until incorporated.

Transfer the pumpkin mixture to a bowl and stir in the chia seeds, plus ½ cup (50 g) of graham cracker crumbs until combined. Place 24 tablespoon-sized (15 g) scoops onto a large baking sheet and freeze the donut holes for 15 minutes.

Place the remaining graham cracker crumbs in a small bowl, and gently roll the firmer donut holes between your hands for a smoother sphere. Place the donut holes in the crumb bowl to coat them, and then place them on a plate; they will be fairly soft. Serve with cream cheese dipping sauce. Store the donut holes in the refrigerator for up to 1 week.

FOR THE CREAM CHEESE DIPPING SAUCE:

In a small bowl, whisk together the vegan cream cheese and maple syrup until smooth.

YIELD: 24 DONUT HOLES

NOTE: IT CAN BE HARD TO FIND GRAHAM CRACKERS THAT DON'T HAVE HONEY IN THEM! THERE IS A GLUTEN-FREE GRAHAM CRACKER BRAND THAT I'VE FOUND IN SOME NATURAL FOODS STORES THAT ARE TOTALLY VEGAN AND WORK GREAT IN RECIPES.

CHAPTER 3

PREP-AHEAD RECIPES

DRIED SNACKS, OVERNIGHT DISHES, AND JARS GALORE!

These recipes keep you one step ahead and prepared for nearly anything. Don't have time to make breakfast in the morning? Overnight oats, it is! Is your brain foggy when you get home from work? The Millet Sweet Potato Soup Bags have you covered.

TROPICAL TRAIL MIX

• UNDER 10 INGREDIENTS • 30 MINUTES OR LESS • PORTABLE • MAKE AHEAD
• GLUTEN FREE • OIL FREE

If you need an amazing snack for hiking or traveling, this mix of sweet, tropical fruits and salty coconut-crusted cashews is sure to please! Pack single servings into small jars, tins, or reusable bags for easy trekking.

1 cup (140 g) raw cashews

1 tablespoon (15 ml) maple syrup

3 tablespoons (15 g) unsweetened shredded coconut

Pinch of salt

1 cup (75 g) unsweetened dried mango pieces

1 cup (85 g) banana chips

½ cup (75 g) dried blueberries

½ cup (65 g) dried diced pineapple

Preheat the oven to 350°F (180°C, or gas mark 4) and have ready a small baking sheet or ovenproof dish lined with parchment paper or foil.

In a small bowl, combine the cashews and maple syrup together until evenly coated. Add the shredded coconut and salt to the mixture, and combine again. Spread the mixture out on a baking sheet in one layer. Bake for 9 to 10 minutes, or until golden, stirring halfway through.

Once toasted, cool on a rack for 15 minutes. After the cashews have cooled, place them in a large mixing bowl. Tear the mango into bite-sized pieces, and add them, the banana chips, blueberries, and pineapple to the mixing bowl.

Fold together until combined and store in a cool, dry area until ready to eat. This mix will keep for up to 3 weeks.

YIELD: 8 SERVINGS

OVERNIGHT CHIA SEED PUDDING

• UNDER 10 INGREDIENTS • PORTABLE • MAKE AHEAD • ONE PAN
• GLUTEN FREE • SOY FREE • NUT FREE • OIL FREE

One of my favorite breakfasts that can also pass as a healthy snack is chia pudding! It's super versatile—you can make it any flavor and add whatever you want, and it's almost guaranteed that it'll be tasty. In this case, a simple vanilla-cinnamon pudding topped with apples and pumpkin seeds really hits the spot.

2 cups (475 ml) unsweetened nondairy milk
2 tablespoons (30 ml) agave nectar
1 teaspoon vanilla extract
½ teaspoon ground cinnamon
Pinch of salt
½ cup (80 g) chia seeds
1 cup (120 g) diced apples, divided
2 tablespoons (20 g) pumpkin seeds

Divide the nondairy milk, agave nectar, vanilla, cinnamon, and salt between two 16-ounce (475 ml) jars. Cover the jars with secure lids and shake to combine. Divide the chia seeds and ½ cup (60 g) of apples between the jars, and shake once more.

Leave the jars in the refrigerator overnight or for at least 1 hour. When ready to serve, divide the remaining apples and the pumpkin seeds between the jars and enjoy!

YIELD: 2 SERVINGS

OVERNIGHT PEACH PECAN OATS

• UNDER 10 INGREDIENTS • PORTABLE • MAKE AHEAD • ONE PAN
• GLUTEN FREE • SOY FREE • OIL FREE

Cold oats may sound a little odd, but they are quite enjoyable during warmer seasons—especially when they are as easy to prep as these. Fresh, juicy peaches go wonderfully with the chopped pecans and a hint of nutmeg.

1½ cups (355 ml) unsweetened nondairy milk
2 tablespoons (30 ml) maple syrup
1 teaspoon vanilla extract
Pinch of ground nutmeg
Pinch of salt
1 cup (110 g) gluten-free rolled oats
1 cup (200 g) sliced peaches
½ cup (100 g) chopped pecans

Divide the nondairy milk, maple syrup, vanilla, nutmeg, and salt between two 16-ounce (475 ml) jars. Cover the jars with secure lids and shake to combine. Divide the oats between the jars and shake once more.

Top with peach slices and chopped pecans. Refrigerate overnight or for at least 4 hours. Serve chilled, or microwave to reheat, which I like to do on cold mornings.

YIELD: 2 SERVINGS

BBQ KALE CHIPS

• UNDER 10 INGREDIENTS • 30 MINUTES OR LESS • PORTABLE • MAKE AHEAD
• GLUTEN FREE • SOY FREE • NUT FREE

When I first got my dehydrator, the first recipe I made was kale chips! Ever since then, I make sure to get a batch going when I have some sad-looking kale in the fridge. For this flavor-bomb of a recipe, you don't need a dehydrator, just an oven, but you'll get the same crispy goodness from it.

3 tablespoons (50 g) tomato paste
1 tablespoon (15 ml) olive oil
1 tablespoon (15 ml) maple syrup
1 tablespoon (5 g) nutritional yeast
2 teaspoons (5 g) onion powder
1 teaspoon smoked paprika
1 teaspoon salt
½ teaspoon garlic powder
⅛ teaspoon cayenne pepper
½ pound (230 g) curly kale, stems removed

Preheat the oven to 350°F (180°C, or gas mark 4), and line two baking sheets with parchment paper.

In a large mixing bowl, whisk together the tomato paste, olive oil, maple syrup, nutritional yeast, onion powder, smoked paprika, salt, garlic powder, and cayenne pepper until combined. Tear the curly kale into bite-sized pieces, adding them to the bowl.

Using your hands, massage the marinade into the kale until evenly coated, then spread the kale pieces over the parchment paper in a single layer. The pieces do not need much space between them, as they will shrink when baked.

Bake for 7 minutes, then switch baking sheet positions and bake for an additional 7 minutes, or until the chips start to brown and are no longer damp. Eat right out of the oven or allow the chips to cool for 20 to 30 minutes before putting them in a jar or bag with a moisture-absorbing packet.

YIELD: 4 SMALL SERVINGS

NOTE: I LOVE USING CURLY KALE FOR KALE CHIPS BECAUSE ALL THE EXTRA FOLDS REALLY ADD TO THE CRUNCH FACTOR, BUT YOU CAN USE WHATEVER KALE YOU HAVE AVAILABLE TO YOU!

ACORN SQUASH CHIPS

• UNDER 10 INGREDIENTS • PORTABLE • MAKE AHEAD
• GLUTEN FREE • SOY FREE • NUT FREE • SUGAR FREE

These squash chips are a fun and healthier alternative to your standard potato chips. Baked instead of fried, and with a subtly sweet flavor, they travel a bit better than kale chips, so they're better for taking with you when you are on the go.

12 ounces (350 g) acorn squash
1 tablespoon (15 ml) sunflower oil
1 teaspoon dried thyme
½ teaspoon salt
½ teaspoon ground mustard seed
¼ teaspoon white pepper

Preheat the oven to 300°F (150°C, or gas mark 2), and line a baking sheet with parchment paper.

Cut your acorn squash in half lengthwise and scoop out the seeds. You can discard the seeds or save them to roast later. Slice your squash into ⅛-inch (3 mm) thick half-moons, and place them in a large mixing bowl.

Drizzle oil over the squash, and sprinkle thyme, salt, mustard seed, and white pepper over as well. Gently toss the squash until evenly coated, then spread it out in a single layer over the parchment paper. Bake for 20 minutes, then carefully flip each slice over, baking for an additional 20 to 30 minutes, or until the pieces are golden brown.

Take the baking sheet out and sprinkle the chips with salt. You can serve the chips right away or cool on a rack for 20 to 30 minutes before putting them in a jar or bag with a moisture-absorbing packet.

YIELD: 4 SERVINGS

NOTE: YOU CAN TRY THIS RECIPE WITH THE SAME QUANTITY OF OTHER SQUASH, SUCH AS BUTTERNUT, KABOCHA, OR DELICATA. BAKING TIMES MAY VARY DEPENDING ON IF THE SQUASH SLICES ARE SMALLER OR LARGER.

RAINBOW FRUIT SMOOTHIE JARS

• UNDER 10 INGREDIENTS • 30 MINUTES OR LESS • PORTABLE • MAKE AHEAD
• GLUTEN FREE • SOY FREE • NUT FREE • OIL FREE • SUGAR FREE

Minutes matter when it comes to shaving off seconds of sleep before work. Fast and easy, you can prep these smoothie jars on Sunday, so that they can make your weekday morning routine simpler, while starting you off with a refreshing breakfast.

2 cups (200 g) frozen spinach

2 cups (300 g) frozen pineapple

2 cups (300 g) chopped oranges, seeds and peel removed

2 cups (250 g) frozen strawberries

2 tablespoons (18 g) chia seeds

4 cups (950 ml) water, coconut water, or unsweetened nondairy milk

Divide the spinach, pineapple, oranges, strawberries, and chia seeds between four 16-ounce (475-ml) jars. Keep in the freezer until ready to prepare the smoothies.

Once you are ready to make one, dump one jar's contents into a blender, along with 1 cup (235 ml) of water, and blend until smooth. You may need to add more water, to help blend, depending on your blender; or you can thaw the ingredients in the jar for 15 minutes before blending.

Repeat the process with the remaining smoothie jars.

YIELD: 4 SMOOTHIES

TIP: YOU CAN CUSTOMIZE THE FRUITS IN THIS SMOOTHIE DEPENDING ON YOUR PREFERENCES. TRY IT OUT WITH BANANAS INSTEAD OF PINEAPPLE AND CHERRIES INSTEAD OF STRAWBERRIES, OR WHATEVER YOU'RE INTO!

VANILLA CHIP BUCKWHEAT BARS

• UNDER 10 INGREDIENTS • PORTABLE • MAKE AHEAD • ONE PAN
• GLUTEN FREE • SOY FREE • NUT FREE • OIL FREE

Protein and snack bars are a lifesaver for me when traveling, but some are filled with all kinds of wild ingredients that are hard to recognize. Here, I have for you bars that are made with whole ingredients, travel easily, and are filling when hunger strikes.

1 cup (180 g) buckwheat groats
2 cups (475 ml) water
2 cups (230 g) gluten-free rolled oats
1 cup (130 g) pitted dates
¼ cup (60 ml) agave nectar
1 teaspoon vanilla extract
½ teaspoon salt
1 cup (160 g) vegan chocolate chips
½ cup (40 g) unsweetened shredded coconut

TIP: TRY ADDING A SCOOP OF YOUR FAVORITE VEGAN PROTEIN POWDER TO THIS RECIPE TO BUMP UP THE PROTEIN CONTENT!

Preheat the oven to 350°F (180°C, or gas mark 4), and line a baking sheet with parchment paper.

In a small pot, bring the buckwheat groats and water to a simmer over medium-low heat. Cook the grains for 5 to 7 minutes, uncovered, until tender. Strain off any excess liquid, allow it to cool for 10 minutes, then place the buckwheat in a food processor with the oats, dates, agave nectar, vanilla, and salt. Pulse until the mixture is combined, and the oats and dates are slightly broken down.

Fold the chocolate chips and coconut into the bar mixture until evenly mixed, then spread the mixture out into a 9 x 12-inch (23 x 30 cm) rectangle, ½-inch (1.25 cm) high. Using a pizza cutter or knife, cut twelve 2.5 x 4-inch (6.25 x 10 cm) bars out of the rectangle without separating them.

Bake the bars for 30 minutes, then flip them, separating the bars at their perforations. Bake for 15 minutes until they begin to brown around the edges. Cool on a rack for 15 minutes for serving, or for 45 minutes before putting them into a container with a moisture-absorbing packet.

YIELD: 12 BARS

TERIYAKI MUSHROOM JERKY

• UNDER 10 INGREDIENTS • PORTABLE • MAKE AHEAD
• GLUTEN FREE • SOY-FREE OPTION • NUT FREE • OIL FREE

Though I kind of hate to admit it, one of my favorite road trip snacks from my pre-vegan days was jerky. Re-creating a similar dehydrated texture with great, cruelty-free flavors and foods led me to make this Teriyaki Mushroom Jerky! I'll be making a double batch of this for my next road trip, and after you try it, I think you will, too.

1 pound portobello mushrooms

½ cup (120 ml) Easy Teriyaki Sauce (page 189)

Pinch of salt

Cut the mushrooms into ¼-inch (6 mm) thick slices, then place them in a large zip bag. Cover the slices in Easy Teriyaki Sauce, then close the bag, getting out as much air as possible. Marinate the mushrooms for 1 hour or more.

In the last 10 minutes of marinating, preheat the oven to 300°F (150°C, or gas mark 2), and line a baking sheet with parchment paper. Then place the mushroom slices on the parchment paper in a single layer. Bake for 35 minutes. Flip the pieces over, sprinkle with a pinch of salt, and bake for an additional 35 minutes, or until they have greatly reduced in size and start to brown around the edges.

Cool the baking sheets on a rack for 20 to 30 minutes before serving the jerky or putting it in a jar or bag with a moisture-absorbing packet for later snacking. Jerky can also be stored in the refrigerator for up to 2 weeks.

YIELD: 4 SERVINGS

SMOKY PARMESAN POPCORN

• UNDER 10 INGREDIENTS • 30 MINUTES OR LESS • PORTABLE • MAKE AHEAD • ONE PAN
• GLUTEN FREE • SOY-FREE OPTION • NUT FREE • SUGAR FREE

One of my mom's favorite snacks is popcorn, so I dedicate this recipe to her! While she has a spiffy popcorn maker, it's just as easy to make this savory, spicy snack in a pot on your stovetop. The combination of chipotle, smoked paprika, and my Sunflower Parmesan (page 193) really take this humble snack to the next level!

3 tablespoons (45 ml) sunflower oil

¾ teaspoon salt, divided

½ cup (105 g) popcorn kernels

1½ tablespoons (25 ml) melted soy-free vegan butter

3 tablespoons (20 g) Sunflower Parmesan (page 193)

½ teaspoon smoked paprika

¼ teaspoon chipotle powder

Warm the sunflower oil and ½ teaspoon of salt in a large pot over medium-high heat. Once a drop of water sizzles in the pot, add three popcorn kernels to the oil. Once they have popped, add the remaining popcorn kernels and cover the pot with a lid.

When nearly all the kernels are popped, remove the pot from the heat and set aside for the remainder to pop. Drizzle vegan butter over the top, tossing the popcorn to coat it evenly. Sprinkle Sunflower Parmesan, smoked paprika, chipotle powder and ¼ teaspoon of salt over the popcorn, and toss again to coat. Serve warm, or allow to cool before placing in small bags for future snacks.

YIELD: 6 SERVINGS

WHITE BEAN ROSEMARY HUMMUS

• UNDER 10 INGREDIENTS • 30 MINUTES OR LESS • PORTABLE • MAKE AHEAD • ONE PAN
• GLUTEN FREE • SOY FREE • NUT FREE • SUGAR FREE

Making hummus at home is stunningly easy, so if you haven't tried it yourself, this is the perfect recipe to start with. White beans are extra creamy, and you do not have to peel the skins off them like you would with chickpeas, so they make for a silky-smooth hummus.

2 cans (30 ounces, or 850 g) white beans, drained, ¼ cup (55 ml) liquid reserved

2 tablespoons (30 ml) tahini

2 tablespoons (30 ml) lemon juice

1 tablespoon (15 ml) olive oil, plus ½ teaspoon for topping

1 tablespoon (2 g) fresh rosemary, or more to taste

2 cloves garlic, peeled

¾ teaspoon salt, or to taste

½ teaspoon lemon zest

¼ teaspoon black pepper, or more to taste

Place all the ingredients in a food processor, and process with an S-blade until completely smooth. Taste the hummus and add more salt, pepper, or rosemary to your preference, if necessary. You can serve immediately, though I feel refrigerating for 30 minutes yields the best results.

Transfer the hummus to a serving bowl and drizzle with ½ teaspoon of olive oil. Serve with crackers, fresh veggies, or pita chips. Hummus will last up to 10 days in a refrigerator.

YIELD: 16 SMALL SERVINGS

HERBED ALMOND FLAX CRACKERS

• UNDER 10 INGREDIENTS • PORTABLE • MAKE AHEAD

• GLUTEN FREE • SOY FREE • SUGAR FREE

I feel as though I'm pretty open about the fact that I love snacks. If I don't have plenty of fresh ingredients or leftovers on hand, my meals start to resemble what could be very odd sampler platters. Therefore, I've included these delicious crackers in this chapter! They're heartier than your average cracker, so take them with you or serve them at home with some White Bean Rosemary Hummus (page 60).

1 cup (80 g) almond flour

1 cup (135 g) gluten-free all-purpose flour

½ cup (55 g) ground flaxseed

¼ cup (35 g) sesame seeds

1 teaspoon salt

½ teaspoon black pepper

½ teaspoon dried basil

½ teaspoon dried parsley

½ teaspoon dried oregano

½ teaspoon dried rosemary

¾ cup (175 ml) water

2 tablespoons (30 ml) olive oil

¼ teaspoon coarse sea salt

Preheat the oven to 350°F (180°C, or gas mark 4), and line a baking sheet with parchment paper or a silicone baking mat.

In a mixing bowl, combine the almond flour, gluten-free all-purpose flour, flaxseed, sesame seeds, salt, black pepper, basil, parsley, oregano, and rosemary until combined. Make a well in the dry mix, then pour the water and olive oil into it. Fold the mixture together until there are no dry spots.

Spread the cracker mixture into a 10 x 16-inch (25 x 4 cm) rectangle over the parchment, lightly scoring 8 columns and 5 rows into it with a knife or pizza cutter. Poke a few holes in the top of each cracker and sprinkle with coarse sea salt. Bake for 20 minutes, then flip the crackers over, baking for another 20 minutes, or until edges begin to brown.

Cool the baking sheets on a rack for 20 minutes before serving the crackers, or 30 minutes before putting them in a jar or bag with a moisture-absorbing packet for later snacking. The crackers will last for 2 to 3 weeks when stored in a cool, dry area.

YIELD: 4 SERVINGS

TIP: IF YOU ARE HAVING A HARD TIME SPREADING THE CRACKER DOUGH OUT WITH A SPATULA, TRY PLACING ANOTHER PIECE OF PARCHMENT OVER THE TOP AND ROLLING IT OUT TO SIZE.

BANANA NUT PROTEIN BITES

• UNDER 10 INGREDIENTS • 30 MINUTES OR LESS • PORTABLE • MAKE AHEAD
• GLUTEN FREE • SOY FREE • OIL FREE • SUGAR FREE

Protein bites are super convenient in that you can have them on hand for a long run or bicycle ride, or enjoy a couple as a healthy, post-workout treat. Bananas and dates give you a boost of potassium, while the pepitas and walnuts provide proteins and healthy fats. Adding cinnamon and vanilla to the mix really brings out those banana nut bread flavors, which makes these bites special.

1 cup (185 g) sliced bananas

1 cup (105 g) walnut halves

1 cup (130 g) roasted pepitas
    (shelled pumpkin seeds), divided

¼ cup (40 g) ground flaxseed

3 Medjool dates, pitted

¼ teaspoon ground cinnamon

¼ teaspoon vanilla extract

Pinch of salt

TIP: TO ADD A POP OF COLOR AND EVEN MORE NUTRITION, TRY MIXING 1 TABLESPOON (10 G) OF YOUR FAVORITE, UNFLAVORED GREENS POWDER INTO THE MIXTURE WHILE PROCESSING.

In a food processor equipped with an S-blade, pulse the bananas, walnuts, ½ cup (65 g) of pepitas, flaxseed, dates, cinnamon, vanilla, and salt together until they make a slightly chunky dough. Do not process too much or you will get a mushy paste.

Make approximately twenty 1-tablespoon-sized (10 g) balls with the dough, and place them on a baking sheet to refrigerate for 10 minutes. Chop the remaining ½ cup (65 g) of pepitas into smaller pieces, then place them in a small bowl. After refrigerating, press each ball into the pepita pieces to crust the outside until each protein bite is covered.

Serve immediately, or store in your refrigerator for up to 10 days for snacking.

YIELD: 20 BITES

FREEZER BLACK BEAN BURRITOS

• PORTABLE • MAKE AHEAD

• GLUTEN-FREE OPTION • SOY FREE • NUT FREE • OIL FREE • SUGAR FREE

Freezer burritos can be a real lifesaver! Because I'm perpetually running late, I like to let a burrito defrost a little on my commute to work. Then I pop it in the microwave—sans foil—and enjoy it with some of my favorite hot sauc

FOR THE RICE:

1 cup (190 g) short-grain brown rice

2 cups (475 ml) water

2 tablespoons (5 g) minced fresh cilantro

2 teaspoons (10 ml) lime juice

½ teaspoon salt

FOR THE BEANS:

2 cans (30 ounces, or 850 g) black beans

1½ teaspoons ground cumin

3 cloves garlic, minced

3 bay leaves

1 teaspoon salt

Pinch of cayenne pepper

FOR THE VEGGIES:

½ cup (70 g) diced red bell pepper

1 cup (175 g) cooked corn kernels

½ cup (70 g) finely diced red onion

FOR THE ASSEMBLY:

4 large whole wheat flour tortillas or 8 small gluten-free tortillas

2 cups (100 g) chopped romaine

1 large avocado, sliced

1 tablespoon (15 ml) hot sauce, for topping (optional)

TIP: IF YOU DON'T LIKE THE IDEA OF WARM AVOCADO, MAKE THE REST OF THE BURRITO. ON THE DAY YOU'LL BE ENJOYING IT, REHEAT THE BURRITO AND ADD FRESH AVOCADO SLICES ON THE SIDE.

TO MAKE THE RICE:

Place the rice and water in a medium-sized saucepan or pot, and bring to a boil over medium heat. Cover with a lid, adjust the heat to low, and simmer for 20 to 25 minutes, or until the rice is tender. Remove the lid to allow the rice to dry out slightly, then fold the cilantro, lime juice, and salt into it. Set aside until ready to assemble.

TO MAKE THE BEANS:

Drain and rinse one can of beans, and use the entirety of the second can. Place both in a small pot, along with the cumin, garlic, bay leaves, salt, and cayenne pepper. Bring to a simmer over medium-low heat. Simmer for 15 minutes, uncovered, stirring occasionally.

TO MAKE THE VEGGIES:

In a small bowl, place the bell peppers, corn, and red onions. Toss together until combined.

TO ASSEMBLE:

Microwave the tortillas for 30 seconds to soften them and make them more pliable. Remove the bay leaves from the beans. Divide the rice, beans, veggies, romaine, and avocado between the tortillas. Fold two sides of the tortilla toward the middle, then roll the end closest to you over the filling. Keep rolling until the burrito is completely closed. Wrap in foil and freeze for later.

To reheat, remove the foil and microwave on a microwave-safe plate for 2 minutes, then flip over and heat for 2 more minutes if needed. You can also reheat in an oven or toaster oven by leaving the foil on and baking at 350°F (180°C, or gas mark 4) for 15 to 20 minutes, or until cooked all the way through. Serve with optional hot sauce.

YIELD: 4 BURRITOS

APPLE CRANBERRY GRANOLA

• UNDER 10 INGREDIENTS • 30 MINUTES OR LESS • PORTABLE • MAKE AHEAD
• GLUTEN FREE • SOY FREE • OIL FREE

Making homemade granola is easier than you think, and this apple cranberry blend will keep hunger at bay whether you are traveling via plane or hiking around a beautiful mountain. Using almond butter eliminates the need for the oil that is found in so many store-bought granolas, and it adds even more of that great almond flavor to the chopped nuts.

2 cups (235 g) gluten-free rolled oats
½ cup (65 g) chopped raw almonds
1 cup (86 g) chopped dried apple rings
½ cup (65 g) dried cranberries
2 tablespoons (20 g) chia seeds
½ teaspoon ground cinnamon
¼ teaspoon salt
⅓ cup (85 g) almond butter
⅓ cup (80 ml) maple syrup
1 teaspoon vanilla extract

Preheat the oven to 350°F (180°C, or gas mark 4), and line a baking sheet with parchment paper. In a large mixing bowl, toss the oats, almonds, dried apple, cranberries, chia seeds, cinnamon, and salt together.

In a small bowl, whisk together the almond butter, maple syrup, and vanilla until combined. Pour the wet mixture over the dry mixture, and fold together until everything is evenly coated. Spread the granola out over the baking sheet and bake for 10 to 12 minutes, stirring halfway through. Once the granola is light golden, it is done baking.

Allow the granola to cool on a rack for 10 minutes before breaking into smaller pieces. You can eat it right away, or place it in a jar or bag with a folded paper towel or a moisture-absorbing packet. It will last for 2 to 3 weeks.

YIELD: 6 CUPS (580 G)

MILLET SWEET POTATO SOUP BAGS

• UNDER 10 INGREDIENTS • 30 MINUTES OR LESS • PORTABLE • MAKE AHEAD • ONE PAN
• GLUTEN FREE • SOY FREE • NUT FREE • OIL FREE • SUGAR FREE

While you can make almost any of your favorite soups into handy soup bags, I love the simple, hearty ingredients in the recipe below. Sturdy sweet potatoes and carrots hold up to freezing and reheating, as do collard greens (especially compared to the softer leaves of spinach). You can store these in your freezer or divide them up for easy, single-serving camping meals.

4 cups (235 ml) vegetable broth, divided

1 cup (140 g) diced yellow onion

1 pound (453 g) sweet potatoes, peeled

2 large carrots, sliced

¾ cup (150 g) millet

2 cups (475 ml) water

2 cups (80 g) chopped collard greens
   or similar hearty greens

1 teaspoon dried sage

½ teaspoon dried thyme

¼ teaspoon black pepper

1 teaspoon salt, or to taste

In a large soup pot, add ½ cup (120 ml) of vegetable broth and bring to a simmer over medium heat. Add the yellow onions to the broth, sautéing for 5 minutes, or until they are mostly translucent. Next, add the sweet potatoes and carrots to the pot, cover with a lid, and simmer for 3 minutes.

Add the millet, water, and remaining broth to the pot. Adjust the heat to medium-low, and simmer for 12 to 15 minutes, or until the millet is almost cooked through. Stir the collard greens, sage, thyme, and black pepper into the soup. Cook for 5 minutes, until the greens have reduced in size and are tender. Lastly, season with salt, to taste.

Serve warm, or take the soup off the heat and allow to cool for 20 minutes before dividing among 4 quart-sized (946 ml) bags, and freezing flat. To reheat, remove a bag from the freezer and run water over the outside to loosen the bag. Pour the contents into a pot and bring to a simmer, then serve.

YIELD: 4 SERVINGS

CHAPTER 4

LUNCH BOX STUFFERS

FOR MAKING YOUR COWORKERS KALE-GREEN WITH ENVY

Being that I transitioned from simple PB&Js as a child, to greasy pizza as a high schooler, and then to frozen meals as an adult, I can guarantee you that these lunches will avoid some serious sadness. There are twists on old favorites, as well as fun recipes that you wouldn't expect.

BBQ TEMPEH WRAP

• UNDER 10 INGREDIENTS • 30 MINUTES OR LESS • PORTABLE • MAKE AHEAD
• NUT FREE • SUGAR FREE

You can't have lunch without a wrap option, am I right? But, don't worry, this wrap is not the standard veggie wrap you may find as the only vegan option at your local deli! Here, we've got tempeh covered in barbecue sauce, mixed in with a cool slaw, sweet potatoes, and more greens for a well-rounded lunch.

½ pound (230 g) sweet potato, chopped

2 packages (16 ounces, or 454 g) tempeh, chopped

¾ cup (195 g) vegan barbecue sauce

2 cups (155 g) shredded green cabbage

⅓ cup (30 g) thinly sliced red onion

¼ cup (65 g) Garlic Mayo (page 193)

⅛ teaspoon dried parsley

⅛ teaspoon dried dill

Pinch of salt

4 large tortillas

2 cups (80 g) chopped kale or collard greens

Steam the tempeh and sweet potatoes for 5 to 7 minutes and then add the tempeh to the steamer basket and steam for another 5 minutes or until the sweet potatoes are fork tender. Transfer the tempeh to a medium saucepan, along with the barbecue sauce. Simmer, uncovered, for 5 minutes.

In a small bowl, toss the green cabbage, red onions, Garlic Mayo, parsley, dill, and salt together until combined. Lay out the 4 tortillas and divide the greens between them. Top with the sweet potatoes, tempeh, and slaw. Wrap up the tortilla by folding two sides of the tortilla toward the middle, then rolling the end closest to you over the filling.

Serve warm, or wrap in foil for later.

YIELD: 4 WRAPS

CHIPOTLE WHITE BEAN SALAD SANDWICH

• 30 MINUTES OR LESS • PORTABLE • MAKE AHEAD
• GLUTEN-FREE OPTION • SOY-FREE OPTION • OIL FREE • SUGAR FREE

White beans are so versatile because they don't have a super strong flavor, and they will take on the flavors of whatever you mix with them. While I love using them for making creamy sauces or dips, they also work well in cold bean salads, like this chipotle version. Cashews are added for extra protein and texture, while greens and bell peppers round out the flavors.

FOR THE CHIPOTLE WHITE BEAN SALAD:

½ cup (56 g) raw cashews, plus hot water for soaking

1 can (15 ounces, or 425 g) white beans, drained and rinsed

¼ cup (40 g) diced red onion

¼ cup (65 g) vegan mayo, soy-free if necessary

2 teaspoons (10 ml) Dijon mustard

¼ teaspoon chipotle powder

¼ teaspoon smoked paprika

¼ teaspoon sea salt, or to taste

⅛ teaspoon chili powder

FOR THE SANDWICH FILLING:

½ cup (100 g) mashed avocado

1 teaspoon (5 ml) lime juice

Pinch of salt

8 slices sandwich bread, gluten-free if necessary

2 cups (40 g) baby arugula, kale, or similar; loosely packed

1 red bell pepper, sliced with seeds and stems removed

1 orange bell pepper, sliced with seeds and stems removed

4 slices vegan Cheddar cheese (optional)

TO MAKE THE CHIPOTLE WHITE BEAN SALAD:

Place the cashews in a small bowl and cover with hot water. Soak for 10 to 15 minutes, or until plump and slightly softened. Drain and dice the cashews. Place them in a mixing bowl with the white beans, red onions, vegan mayo, Dijon mustard, chipotle powder, smoked paprika, sea salt, and chili powder.

Using a fork or potato masher, gently mash the mixture together until the beans are mostly broken down, but still chunky. Taste and add more seasoning as needed. Refrigerate until ready to assemble, knowing the longer it marinates in the refrigerator the stronger the flavors will be.

TO MAKE THE SANDWICHES:

In a small bowl, combine the avocado, lime juice, and salt. Spread avocado mash on one side of 4 pieces of bread. Divide the chipotle white bean salad between the other 4 pieces, then top with baby greens and bell pepper slices. Top with optional vegan Cheddar slice and avocado-spread bread. Serve, or wrap up for later enjoyment.

YIELD: 4 SERVINGS

NOTE: BECAUSE THIS SANDWICH DOES NOT HAVE ANY SUPER WET COMPONENTS IN IT (E.G., SLICED TOMATOES, PICKLES), IT'S GREAT FOR PACKING UP IN A REUSABLE SANDWICH BAG OR WRAPPING IN FOIL. PAIR IT WITH A SIDE OF CARROT STICKS AND HUMMUS, AS WELL AS GRAPES, FOR A WELL-ROUNDED LUNCH.

ANTIPASTO CHOP SALAD

Chop salads are a classic when it comes to business lunches, but here's a fun twist on a traditionally meat- and cheese-heavy salad: a vegan antipasto version! Worlds healthier than the traditional version, this salad is packed with flavors reminiscent of the Mediterranean.

FOR THE DRESSING:

6 tablespoons (90 ml) olive oil

2 tablespoons (30 ml) white vinegar

1 tablespoon (15 ml) lemon juice

1 clove garlic, minced

½ teaspoon Italian herb blend

½ teaspoon salt

⅛ teaspoon sugar

Pinch of black pepper

FOR THE SALAD:

1 can (15 ounces, or 425 g) chickpeas, drained and rinsed

½ pound (225 g) chopped tomatoes

½ cup (60 g) chopped black or green olives

1 can (14 ounces, or 400 g) quartered artichoke hearts, drained

8 ounces (225 g) cubed seitan, store-bought or made from Seitan Two Ways (page 190)

7 ounces (200 g) cubed vegan white cheese

6 cups (345 g) chopped romaine

TO MAKE THE DRESSING:

In a small bowl, whisk the olive oil, white vinegar, lemon juice, garlic, Italian herbs, salt, sugar, and pepper together until emulsified.

TO MAKE THE SALAD:

Divide the dressing between four 24-ounce (710 ml) jars, then layer the salad ingredients in the jars, in the order listed, finishing with the romaine. Close each jar with a tight-fitting lid. When ready to serve, gently shake the jar to coat everything with dressing, then empty into a bowl. Serve chilled.

Salad jars will last up to 1 week in the refrigerator.

YIELD: 4 SERVINGS

TIP: TO MAKE THIS RECIPE GLUTEN-FREE, INSTEAD OF USING SEITAN, SIMMER 8 OUNCES (225 G) TEMPEH IN VEGETABLE BROTH. THEN DRAIN, CHILL, AND CHOP!

GRILL AND CHILL SALAD

• PORTABLE • MAKE AHEAD
• GLUTEN FREE • SOY FREE • NUT FREE • SUGAR FREE

Grill and chill kind of sounds like the perfect descriptor of summer, no? In this salad, you'll be using your grill to impart some smoky flavor to some of my favorite veggies, then turning them into a beautiful jar salad, complete with protein from kidney beans and crisp texture from mixed greens.

FOR THE SALAD:

1 pound (455 g) summer squash, cut into ½-inch (12 mm) thick slices

6 ounces (170 g) radishes, halved

2 red bell peppers, stemmed, halved, and seeded

2 ears corn, shucked

4 ounces (115 g) red pearl onions, peeled

2 cans (30 ounces, or 850 g) kidney beans, drained and rinsed

6 cups (265 g) packaged mixed greens

FOR THE DRESSING:

5 tablespoons (75 ml) olive oil

¼ cup (60 ml) lemon juice

1 tablespoon (5 g) nutritional yeast

½ teaspoon dried basil

¼ teaspoon salt

TO MAKE THE SALAD:

Heat your grill to roughly 375°F (190°C). Grill the squash, radishes, bell peppers, corn ears, and red pearl onions for 5 to 7 minutes, flipping halfway through, or until the vegetables are tender and grill marks are visible. Remove the vegetables from the grill and spread them out on a baking sheet. Refrigerate for 45 minutes, or until chilled. Move on to the dressing while chilling.

TO MAKE THE DRESSING:

In a small bowl, whisk the olive oil, lemon juice, nutritional yeast, dried basil, and salt vigorously until combined and creamy.

TO ASSEMBLE:

Divide the dressing between four 24-ounce (710 ml) jars, then top with kidney beans. Cut the corn from the cobs, and chop the large pepper pieces. Place them in a mixing bowl with the squash, radishes, and pearl onions. Toss together until combined. Top the kidney beans with the grilled vegetable mixture, and lastly, top with mixed greens. Close each jar with a tight-fitting lid. When ready to serve, gently shake the jar to coat everything with dressing, then empty into a bowl. Serve chilled.

Salad jars will last up to 1 week in the refrigerator.

YIELD: 4 SERVINGS

SESAME SOBA SALAD

• 30 MINUTES OR LESS • PORTABLE • MAKE AHEAD
• GLUTEN-FREE OPTION • SUGAR FREE

Soba noodles were probably my first experience with eating pasta cold—outside of macaroni salad! Here we have a much more nutritious option with crunchy vegetables, protein-rich edamame, and tons of flavor in the peanut butter–sesame dressing. Bring this jar salad to work and check out how fast your coworkers will be drooling.

FOR THE SALAD:

4½ ounces (270 g) uncooked soba noodles, gluten-free if necessary

2 cups (325 g) shelled edamame, steamed

1 cup (65 g) grated carrots

1½ cups (105 g) shredded red cabbage

1½ cups (105 g) shredded white cabbage

2 cups (220 g) snap peas

¼ cup (20 g) chopped scallions

¼ cup (10 g) minced fresh cilantro

1 teaspoon black sesame seeds

FOR THE SESAME DRESSING:

3 tablespoons (45 g) creamy peanut butter

3 tablespoons (45 ml) sesame oil

3 tablespoons (45 g) plain nondairy yogurt

2 tablespoons (30 ml) unseasoned rice vinegar

1½ tablespoons (25 g) sriracha or similar garlic chili hot sauce

1 tablespoon (15 ml) tamari

TO MAKE THE SALAD:

Cook the soba noodles according to the package instructions until al dente. Rinse with very cold water, and set aside. While the noodles are cooking, make the dressing.

TO MAKE THE SESAME DRESSING:

In a small bowl, whisk the peanut butter, sesame oil, nondairy yogurt, rice vinegar, sriracha, and tamari together until combined.

TO ASSEMBLE:

Divide the dressing between four 24-ounce (710 ml) jars. Then, divide the edamame, carrots, red cabbage, white cabbage, snap peas, cooked soba noodles, scallions, cilantro, and sesame seeds between the jars, in that order.

Close each jar with a tight-fitting lid and refrigerate. When ready to serve, gently shake the jar to coat everything with dressing, then empty into a bowl. Serve chilled. Salad jars will last up to 1 week in the refrigerator.

YIELD: 4 JARS

KALE RASPBERRY GRAIN SALAD

• UNDER 10 INGREDIENTS • 30 MINUTES OR LESS • MAKE AHEAD • PORTABLE
• GLUTEN FREE • SOY FREE • NUT FREE

If the beautiful color of the raspberry vinaigrette didn't catch your eye, the flavor surely will. This vibrant salad is more on the sweet side than savory, and it is filled will all kinds of flavors and textures. I love the crunch the sunflower seeds provide, and the subtle, refreshing aroma from the mint, which is good buddies with all things raspberry.

2 cups (475 ml) water

1 cup (190 g) white quinoa

⅛ teaspoon salt

1½ cups (240 g) fresh raspberries, divided

¼ cup (60 ml) olive oil

2 tablespoons (30 ml) balsamic vinegar

1 tablespoon (15 ml) agave nectar

1 tablespoon (15 ml) lemon juice

¼ teaspoon poppy seeds

1 bunch lacinato kale, chopped with stems removed

1 tablespoon (3 g) minced fresh mint

½ cup (70 g) sunflower seeds

Place the water, quinoa, and salt in a large pan. Cover with a lid and bring to a boil over medium heat. Reduce the heat to medium-low and simmer for 15 to 18 minutes, then leave the cooked quinoa uncovered for 3 minutes. Toss with a spoon or fork to fluff. Set aside to cool.

While the quinoa is cooking, place ¾ cup (120 g) of raspberries, olive oil, balsamic vinegar, agave nectar, lemon juice, and poppy seeds in a blender. Purée until very smooth.

Once cooled, fold the quinoa, kale, and mint together until combined. To prep the salad in a jar, divide the dressing between four 24-ounce (710 ml) jars, then layer with the remaining raspberries, sunflower seeds, and quinoa mixture. Close each jar with a tight-fitting lid. When ready to serve, gently shake the jar to coat everything. If serving in a bowl, divide the quinoa mixture between 4 bowls, then top with dressing, raspberries, and sunflower seeds.

Salads will last up to 5 days in the refrigerator.

YIELD: 4 SERVINGS

COCONUT BLT + P

• UNDER 10 INGREDIENTS • 30 MINUTES OR LESS • PORTABLE • MAKE AHEAD • ONE PAN
• GLUTEN-FREE OPTION • SOY-FREE OPTION • NUT FREE • OIL FREE

My boyfriend's favorite sandwich—well, aside from a grilled cheese—is a BLT. I only messed with the equation a little bit by using my Coconut Bacon (page 195), vegan mayo, and fresh peach slices, which go together wonderfully.

8 slices sourdough bread (or use gluten free, if necessary)

5 tablespoons (70 g) vegan mayo, soy free if necessary

8 leaves green leaf lettuce

8 thin slices large tomato

1 cup (160 g) sliced peaches

¾ cup (50 g) Coconut Bacon (page 195)

⅛ teaspoon cracked black pepper

Lay out the 8 pieces of bread, and spread roughly 2 teaspoons (9 g) of vegan mayo on one side of each slice. Layer 2 leaves of lettuce, 2 slices of tomato, ¼ cup (40 g) peach slices, 3 tablespoons (4 g) Coconut Bacon, and a pinch of black pepper on 4 of the slices. Then top with the remaining slices of bread.

Serve, or wrap up for your lunch box!

YIELD: 4 SANDWICHES

BAGEL HUMMUS VEGGIE SANDWICH

• UNDER 10 INGREDIENTS • 30 MINUTES OR LESS • PORTABLE • MAKE AHEAD • ONE PAN
• SOY FREE • NUT FREE • SUGAR FREE • OIL FREE

Sometimes, you gotta keep it simple, like with my bagel sandwich. This one is elevated with the use of White Bean Rosemary Hummus (page 60) and veggies to create a beautiful filling between toasted bagels.

4 bagels, sliced in half

1 cup (200 g) White Bean Rosemary Hummus (page 60)

1 cup (25 g) large pieces of kale

1 cup (180 g) thinly sliced tomato

1 cup (150 g) thinly slice red onion

1 cup (170 g) thinly sliced cucumber

1 avocado, sliced (optional)

Toast the bagels until golden brown, or until toasted to preference. Spread 2 tablespoons (12.5 g) hummus onto each cut side of the bagels. Divide the kale, tomato slices, red onions, cucumber, and optional avocado on 4 of the bagel halves. Top with the remaining bagel halves and serve.

YIELD: 4 SANDWICHES

TIP: IF MAKING FOR YOUR NEXT DAY'S LUNCH, TRY REMOVING MOST OF THE SEEDS FROM THE TOMATO SLICES SO THAT THEY DO NOT MAKE THE BAGELS SOGGY.

GRILLED EGGPLANT PESTO PITA POCKETS

• UNDER 10 INGREDIENTS • 30 MINUTES OR LESS • PORTABLE • MAKE AHEAD
• SOY-FREE OPTION • NUT FREE • SUGAR FREE

Three things that I love: grilling, pesto, and pitas, all wrapped up into one delicious lunch box–stuffing recipe! Here, a little prep goes a long way, with a homemade pesto aioli that you will be wanting to spread on everything.

1 pound (455 g) eggplant

1 teaspoon salt

½ teaspoon garlic powder

½ teaspoon ground cumin

Cooking oil spray

¼ cup (60 g) Nut-Free Pepita Pesto (page 198)

¼ cup (60 g) Garlic Mayo (page 193) or vegan mayo, soy free if necessary

2 pitas, cut in half

1 large carrot, cut into matchsticks

2 cups (60 g) baby spinach

1 cup (50 g) sprouts, such as sunflower, pea, or alfalfa

Preheat the grill to 375°F (190°C). Slice the eggplant into ½-inch (1.25 cm) thick rounds, and lay them out on a baking sheet lined with paper towels or a clean kitchen towel. Sprinkle ½ teaspoon of salt over the rounds, then flip them over and sprinkle with the other ½ teaspoon of salt. Wait 15 to 20 minutes for water to seep out of the eggplant.

Brush off as much salt as you can. Sprinkle garlic powder and cumin over the eggplant rounds, then spray them with a light coat of cooking oil spray. Grill the eggplant for 2 to 4 minutes on each side, or until tender and grill marks are dark. Remove from the grill and set aside.

In a small bowl, whisk together the pesto and vegan mayo until combined. Spread 2 tablespoons (30 g) of pesto aioli inside each pita half, then divide the eggplant slices, carrots, spinach, and sprouts between the halves. Serve immediately, or store in a closed container for serving later.

YIELD: 4 SERVINGS

BAKED FALAFEL COLLARD CUPS

• PORTABLE • MAKE AHEAD
• GLUTEN FREE • SOY FREE • OIL FREE

During my time as a product design engineer, I tried my first falafel at a food court during my lunch hour. My life was changed! Thinking back to that time, and all the times I've enjoyed falafel since, I wanted to give you one of my favorite baked falafel recipes, for lunch. And you know that I could not leave you without a vegan tzatziki recipe!

FOR THE BAKED FALAFEL:

½ cup (65 g) gluten-free rolled oats

2 cans (30 ounces, 850 g) chickpeas, drained and rinsed, 2 tablespoons (30 ml) aqua-faba (a.k.a. chickpea brine) reserved

2 cups (80 g) arugula

½ cup (70 g) chopped white onion

1 tablespoon (15 ml) lemon juice

2 cloves garlic, peeled

2 teaspoons (1 g) dried parsley

2 teaspoons (5 g) ground cumin

1 teaspoon ground coriander

1 teaspoon salt

¼ teaspoon paprika

¼ teaspoon black pepper

FOR THE TZATZIKI:

¾ cup (110 g) raw cashews

⅓ cup (80 ml) water

1 tablespoon (15 ml) lemon juice

1 clove garlic, peeled

⅛ teaspoon dried dill

½ teaspoon salt

¾ cup (100 g) grated cucumber

FOR THE QUICK-PICKLED ONIONS:

½ cup (80 g) thinly sliced red onion

1 teaspoon white vinegar

⅛ teaspoon salt

⅛ teaspoon agave nectar

FOR ASSEMBLY:

12 small collard leaves

½ cup (60 g) thinly sliced radishes

TO MAKE THE BAKED FALAFEL:

Preheat the oven to 375°F (190°C, or gas mark 5), and line a large baking sheet with parchment paper or a silicone baking mat. Place the oats in a food processor equipped with an S-blade, and pulse until they resemble coarse bread crumbs.

Add the chickpeas, arugula, white onions, 1 tablespoon (15 ml) of aquafaba, lemon juice, garlic, parsley, cumin, coriander, salt, paprika, and black pepper to the food processor. Pulse until it makes a slightly chunky dough. Do not process too much or it will turn into a paste. Scoop 2-tablespoon-sized (20 g) pucks onto the baking sheet, smoothing them if necessary.

Bake for 12 minutes, flip, and bake for 12 additional minutes, or until the tops are golden.

TO MAKE THE TZATZIKI:

While the falafel is baking, place the raw cashews, water, remaining 1 tablespoon (15 ml) of aquafaba, lemon juice, garlic, dill, and salt in a blender. Purée until mostly smooth, then let it sit for 5 minutes

to absorb moisture to soften the cashews. Add ¼ cup (30 g) of the cucumber and blend again until smooth, folding in the rest of the cucumber until combined. Refrigerate until ready to assemble.

TO MAKE THE QUICK-PICKLED ONIONS:

Place the red onion, white vinegar, salt, and agave nectar in a small bowl. Toss together until evenly mixed. Refrigerate until ready to assemble.

TO ASSEMBLE:

Stack collard green leaves on top of each other and wrap in a damp towel. Microwave for 60 seconds or until the leaves are tender and pliable. Place 3 small collard leaves on 4 plates or containers, then add 2 falafel balls onto each one. Next, top the falafels with tzatziki, pickled onions, and radish slices, then serve.

If you are packing this for lunch, keep the tzatziki on the side as to not turn the falafel into mush.

YIELD: 4 SERVINGS

STUFFED DELI SANDWICH

• UNDER 10 INGREDIENTS • 30 MINUTES OR LESS • PORTABLE • MAKE AHEAD • ONE PAN
• NUT FREE • OIL FREE • SUGAR FREE

If you've ever worked in an office where there was a lunch meeting, you've probably seen platters of deli sandwiches from the local caterer laid out for all the employees. Now, imagine the sandwich is a hundred times better, and it's made cruelty-free! That's this deli sandwich.

4 sub sandwich rolls

¼ cup (60 ml) vegan mayo

4 teaspoons (20 g) Dijon mustard

1 tablespoon (15 ml) red wine vinegar

Pinch of salt

Pinch of pepper

1 pound (455 g) Seitan Two Ways (page 190), thinly sliced

4 ounces (120 g) red leaf lettuce leaves

4 vegan cheese slices, sliced in half, corner to corner

1 cup (180 g) tomato slices, seeds removed

¼ cup (35 g) pickled pepperoncini, sliced

If your sandwich rolls are not cut, slice them down the middle lengthwise. Spread 1 tablespoon (15 g) vegan mayo onto 4 of the roll halves, followed by 1 teaspoon (5 g) Dijon mustard. Drizzle red wine vinegar over the other 4 roll halves, followed by salt and pepper.

On the bottom halves, layer slices of seitan, red leaf lettuce, 2 halves of vegan cheese, tomato slices, and, lastly, pepper-oncini. Cover with top buns and serve or wrap in sandwich paper to enjoy later.

YIELD: 4 SERVINGS

GROWN-UP AB&J

• UNDER 10 INGREDIENTS • 30 MINUTES OR LESS • PORTABLE • MAKE AHEAD • ONE PAN • GLUTEN-FREE OPTION • SOY FREE • OIL FREE

Growing up, PB&Js were a staple in my diet, and something I had in my lunch box on the regular. Now, I don't find myself eating them as much, but when I do it always brings me back. Instead of serving you up the basics, I've turned the volume up on this sandwich with almond butter, homemade jam, some spices, and of course, some banana slices.

8 slices whole wheat bread (or use gluten-free bread, if necessary)
6 tablespoons (95 g) almond butter
2 large bananas, sliced
⅛ teaspoon ground cinnamon
⅛ teaspoon ground cardamom
2 teaspoons (10 ml) agave nectar (optional)
½ cup (140 g) Berry Rhubarb Chia Jam (page 186) or your favorite jelly

Toast the bread slices until light brown, then lay out 4 slices. Spread 1½ tablespoons (24 g) of almond butter onto each of the 4 slices, then top with sliced banana, cinnamon, cardamom, and optional agave nectar. Lastly, spread 2 tablespoons (17 g) of Berry Rhubarb Chia Jam onto the remaining 4 slices of bread and top off the sandwiches.

Serve warm, or forgo the toasting and wrap the sandwiches up for later.

YIELD: 4 SERVINGS

SHIITAKE SPRING ROLLS

• 30 MINUTES OR LESS • PORTABLE • MAKE AHEAD
• GLUTEN FREE • NUT FREE • SUGAR FREE

For a refreshing lunch, spring rolls are where it's at. In this case, we have the traditional fillings of rice noodles and fresh herbs, but we also have a savory mixture of shiitake mushrooms and tempeh for added flavor and protein. I love to dip my spring rolls in sweet Thai chili sauce, but you could also make Sesame Dressing (page 77) as a savory option.

4 ounces (15 g) uncooked rice noodles

1 tablespoon (15 ml) toasted sesame oil

8 ounces (225 g) tempeh, chopped

3 ounces (85 g) shiitake mushrooms, chopped

1½ tablespoons (25 ml) tamari

1 tablespoon (15 ml) lime juice

¼ teaspoon dulse flakes

1 large carrot, julienne-cut

¼ cup (5 g) mint leaves

¼ cup (5 g) cilantro leaves

¼ cup (5 g) basil leaves

8 spring roll wrappers

½ cup (120 ml) sweet Thai chili sauce

8 leaves green lettuce (optional)

Cook the rice noodles according to the package instructions until they are al dente. Drain and rinse them with very cold water, then set aside until ready to assemble.

In a medium pan, warm the sesame oil over medium-high heat. Once hot, add the tempeh and shiitake mushrooms to the pan. Sauté for 5 minutes, or until two or three sides are lightly browned. Adjust the heat to medium-low and stir the tamari, lime juice, and dulse flakes into the tempeh mixture. Simmer for 5 minutes, breaking down the tempeh with a spoon into crumbles.

Transfer the tempeh to a bowl. Rinse the pan out, fill it with 1 inch (2.5 cm) of water, then warm it over low heat. Set out little piles of the tempeh, carrot, mint, cilantro, and basil as filling ingredients for assembling the rolls.

Dunk 1 spring roll wrapper at a time into the warm water for about 5 seconds. Lay it out on a flat surface and place roughly 2 tablespoons (30 g) of tempeh mixture in the center of the wrapper in an almost rectangle shape. Top with a couple pieces of carrot, mint, cilantro, and basil, then a few strands of the rice noodles, and wrap it up by folding in one side of the paper parallel to the filling, then fold the two side panels toward the center, hold it firmly, and roll the rest of it up, pressing down on the seam.

Repeat the process 7 more times until both the filling and the wrappers are used up. Serve immediately with sweet Thai chili sauce for dipping. Or to store for lunch, wrap each spring roll in a leaf of lettuce so that they don't stick together.

YIELD: 8 SPRING ROLLS

VEGGIE SUSHI BENTO BOX

• UNDER 10 INGREDIENTS • 30 MINUTES OR LESS • PORTABLE • MAKE AHEAD
• GLUTEN FREE • SOY-FREE OPTION • NUT FREE • OIL FREE • SUGAR FREE

When I was in college, I really didn't cook—like, at all. Luckily for me, there was a sushi restaurant in the same parking lot as my school, and I went there very frequently. While that habit got expensive quickly, this brown rice roll will satiate your sushi craving without breaking the bank!

2 cups (475 ml) water
1 cup (200 g) short-grain brown rice
2 teaspoons (10 ml) rice vinegar
Pinch of salt
4 sheets nori seaweed
2 ounces (60 g) carrots, julienne-cut
2 ounces (60 g) cucumber, julienne-cut
2 ounces (60 g) mango, peeled and sliced
2 ounces (60 g) avocado, sliced
½ cup (40 g) scallions, cut into 3-inch (7.5-cm) pieces
¼ cup (60 ml) tamari, for serving (optional)

In a covered pot, bring the water, brown rice, rice vinegar, and salt to a boil over medium-high heat. Once boiling, adjust the heat to medium-low. Simmer the rice for 20 to 25 minutes, or until tender and fluffy. Remove from the heat, uncover, fluff with a wooden spoon, and cool for 10 minutes.

Lay out the 4 sheets of seaweed, then spread the brown rice over half of each sheet. In a line down the middle of the rice, place ½ ounce (15 g) each of the carrots, cucumber, mango, and avocado, then top with 2 tablespoons (10 g) of scallions.

Pick up the rice-end of the nori sheet, carefully cover the filling, and pull it taut, making sure that the rice sticks together and the filling does not move. Continue to roll the seaweed until there is ½ inch (1.25 cm) left, then dampen the edge with wet fingertips. Press the edge down and make sure that the seam is sticking, then repeat with the other three rolls.

Either place each roll whole in a lunch box, or slice them into 8 sushi pieces and serve with a side of tamari.

YIELD: 4 SERVINGS

TIP: MAKE THIS LUNCH COMPLETE BY SERVING IT WITH SIDES OF SNAP PEAS AND BAKED TOFU, FOR SOME ADDED PROTEIN!

WHOLE WHEAT EMPANADAS

• PORTABLE • MAKE AHEAD
• SOY FREE • NUT FREE • SUGAR FREE

If you have never had an empanada before, they are like a South American hot pocket. Typically, you can find them with non-vegan fillings, but here I have filled them with seasoned Buckwheat Taco Meat (page 185), along with mixed vegetables and golden raisins to provide little pops of sweetness.

FOR THE CRUST:

¾ cup (90 g) unbleached all-purpose flour
½ cup (60 g) whole wheat pastry flour
¼ cup (40 g) cornmeal
2 teaspoons (9 g) baking powder
1 teaspoon salt
1 teaspoon onion powder
½ cup (120 ml) water
2 tablespoons (30 ml) olive oil

FOR THE FILLING AND ASSEMBLY:

1 tablespoon (15 ml) sunflower oil
½ cup (70 g) diced red onion
1 cup (150 g) diced green bell pepper
2 cloves garlic, minced
2 cups (350 g) Buckwheat Taco Meat
    (page 185)
2 cups (80 g) baby spinach
¼ cup (50 g) golden raisins
¼ cup (7 g) cilantro leaves
½ cup (55 g) vegan Cheddar shreds
    (optional)
Pinch of salt, or to taste
1 tablespoon (15 ml) aquafaba
    (a.k.a. chickpea brine)

TO MAKE THE CRUST:

In a large mixing bowl, sift the all-purpose flour, whole wheat flour, cornmeal, baking powder, salt, and onion powder together until combined. Make a well in the center of the dry ingredients, add the water and olive oil, then knead for 1 minute, making sure there are no dry spots. Set aside until ready to assemble.

TO MAKE THE FILLING AND ASSEMBLE:

Preheat the oven to 375°F (190°C, or gas mark 5), and line a baking sheet with parchment paper.

Warm the oil in a skillet over medium heat and once hot, add the red onions and bell peppers to the pan. Sauté the mixture for 3 minutes, then add the garlic and sauté for an additional minute, or until the onions are mostly translucent. Add the Buckwheat Taco Meat, spinach, raisins, cilantro, and optional Cheddar shreds to the skillet. Cook until the spinach is wilted, about 2 minutes. Season the filling with a pinch of salt, or to taste.

Sprinkle flour over a flat work surface, and divide the dough into 6 equal balls. Roll one dough ball out to 6 inches (15 cm) wide, then place ½ cup (90 g) of filling in the center. Fold and lightly stretch the crust over the filling to create a half-moon shape. Seal ½ inch (15 mm) of the edges by pressing on them with fork tines or pinching them with your fingers.

Repeat with the other 5 dough balls, placing the finished empanadas on the baking sheet. Lastly, brush the tops with aquafaba and bake for 20 minutes, or until they become golden brown around the edges. Serve warm, or let the empanadas cool on a rack for 30 minutes before packing away for lunch.

YIELD: 6 EMPANADAS

CHAPTER 5

MEALS IN 30 MINUTES OR LESS

HOME-COOKED MEALS FOR THE HANGRY

In the time it takes you to wait for a table at your favorite restaurant, you could have one of these stellar meals on your table! Hearty grains, lots of flavor, and you don't have to wait for refills on your drink. Now to figure out who's doing the dishes.

ONE-POT PASTA

When I think of one-pot pasta, it reminds me of slow cooker meals, but done in a timely manner. I say this because all you have to do for this tasty meal is throw every ingredient in a large pot, cover it, and cook for nearly 20 minutes. Yes, 20 minutes! That's nearly a third of my commute to work some days, so this dish is extra convenient.

8 ounces (225 g) whole wheat spaghetti noodles, (or use gluten free pasta if necessary)

3 to 4 cups (720 to 960 ml) water

1 can (15 ounces, or 425 g) tomato sauce

1 can (15 ounces, or 425 g) diced tomatoes

2 cups (80 g) chopped curly kale

½ cup (100 g) halved artichoke hearts

½ cup (90 g) red lentils

¼ cup (30 g) chopped Kalamata olives

Three 3-inch (7.5 cm) rosemary sprigs

1 tablespoon (10 g) capers

3 cloves garlic, minced

¼ teaspoon crushed red pepper

½ teaspoon salt, or to taste

In a large, wide pot, place all the ingredients except the salt. Cover with a lid and bring to a boil over medium heat. Once boiling, adjust the heat to medium-low, and simmer for 15 to 20 minutes, stirring occasionally, until the lentils and pasta are cooked.

If the pot looks dry before the lentils are done cooking, add ½ cup (120 ml) of water at a time, but do not add too much and make it a soup.

Once everything is cooked, season with salt to taste and serve.

YIELD: 4 SERVINGS

SHEET PAN SQUASH TACOS

- 30 MINUTES OR LESS
- GLUTEN FREE • SOY FREE • NUT FREE • SUGAR FREE

Some of my favorite meals to make are sheet pan meals! Chop, toss, roast, and voilà, you have a complete meal with very little active time and even less dishes. These tacos have a wonderful variety of textures and flavors, plus they are perfect for a weeknight dinner.

2 cups (270 g) diced and peeled butternut squash

2 cups (160 g) chopped baby bella mushrooms

1 can (15 ounces, or 425 g) black beans, drained and rinsed

1 cup (160 g) chopped yellow onion

1 tablespoon (15 ml) sunflower oil

1 teaspoon chili powder

½ teaspoon ground cumin

½ teaspoon salt, or more to taste

¼ teaspoon dried oregano

¼ teaspoon paprika

Pinch of cayenne pepper

2 cups (295 g) chopped tomatillos, with husks removed

8 corn tortillas

1 cup (55 g) shredded cabbage

1 jalapeño, thinly sliced

8 small lime wedges

Preheat the oven to 400°F (200°C, or gas mark 6), and line a baking sheet with parchment paper or a silicone mat.

Place the butternut squash, mushrooms, black beans, and yellow onions in a mixing bowl. Drizzle with oil and toss to coat, then add the chili powder, cumin, salt, oregano, paprika, and cayenne pepper, and toss again. Spread the mixture out on the baking sheet, leaving some space for the tomatillos.

Place the tomatillos on the remainder of the baking sheet, then place in the oven for 15 to 20 minutes, or until the squash is fork tender. Sprinkle with more salt to taste, if desired.

Warm the tortillas in either the microwave or on a hot pan until soft and pliable. Fill each one with some butternut–black bean mixture, then top with tomatillos, shredded cabbage, and jalapeño slices. Serve warm, accompanied by lime wedges.

YIELD: 4 SERVINGS

NOTE: BE SURE THAT THE SQUASH IS DICED—NOT CHOPPED. IT IS ESSENTIAL TO MAKING THIS RECIPE QUICK. THE LARGER THE DICE ON THE SQUASH, THE LONGER IT WILL TAKE TO ROAST!

SUMMER STEW

Even if you don't have your own garden, you have probably known someone who was inundated with tomatoes and zucchini once summer came around. This stew uses much of the produce that summer has to offer, such as zucchini, green beans, tomatoes, and corn, and it does so quickly and deliciously! I love serving this with a basket of toasted, crusty bread on the table.

1 tablespoon (15 ml) sunflower oil

1 cup (140 g) diced onion

2 cups (280 g) chopped zucchini

4 ounces (120 g) green beans

2 cloves garlic, minced

3 cups (500 g) chopped tomatoes

1½ cups (315 g) corn kernels

2 cans (30 ounces, or 850 g) white beans, including liquid

1 cup (235 ml) low-sodium vegetable broth

1 teaspoon dried basil, or more to taste

½ teaspoon dried parsley, or more to taste

⅛ teaspoon black pepper, or more to taste

Pinch of crushed red pepper (optional)

1 teaspoon salt, or to taste

Warm the oil in a large pot over medium heat. Once hot, add the onions, zucchini, and green beans to the pot, sautéing for 5 minutes or until the onions are mostly translucent. Next, stir the garlic, tomatoes, and corn into the vegetables, sautéing for 3 more minutes.

Add the white beans plus their liquid, vegetable broth, basil, parsley, black pepper, and optional red pepper to the pot. Simmer, covered, over medium-low heat for 7 minutes, stirring occasionally. Taste the stew and season with salt, plus more herbs if you prefer. Serve hot.

YIELD: 4 SERVINGS

TIP: AT CERTAIN GROCERY STORES YOU CAN BUY GRILLED CORN IN THE FREEZER SECTION. I LOVE THAWING THIS OUT AND USING IT IN RECIPES LIKE THIS ONE TO ADD EVEN MORE FLAVOR.

PINEAPPLE TERIYAKI BURGERS

• 30 MINUTES OR LESS • MAKE AHEAD
• GLUTEN-FREE OPTION • NUT FREE • OIL FREE

There is a time and place for veggie burgers that are stuffed with as many vegetables as possible; this is not one of those times. Here we have a robust patty made mostly of beans and tofu, for a protein-filled teriyaki burger that will satiate almost any intense appetite.

1 can (15 ounces, or 425 g) black beans, drained and rinsed

1 cup (190 g) extra-firm tofu

½ cup (70 g) diced yellow onion

½ cup (120 ml) Easy Teriyaki Sauce (page 189), divided

1 tablespoon (7 g) toasted sesame seeds

2 teaspoons (10 ml) tamari

½ teaspoon liquid smoke

½ teaspoon salt

½ teaspoon garlic powder

½ cup (80 g) brown rice flour

4 pineapple slices, cut ½-inch (1.25 cm) thick, peeled and cored

1 large red onion, cut into ½-inch (1.25 cm) thick slices

4 hamburger buns, gluten-free if necessary

8 leaves butter lettuce

¼ cup (60 g) Garlic Mayo (page 193) or vegan mayo

Preheat the oven to 400°F (200°C, or gas mark 6), and line a baking sheet with parchment paper or a silicone baking mat. Also, preheat a grill to 375°F (190°C).

In a food processor equipped with an S-blade, pulse the black beans, tofu, yellow onions, ¼ cup (60 ml) of Easy Teriyaki Sauce, sesame seeds, tamari, liquid smoke, salt, and garlic powder together until they resemble ground meat. Fold the brown rice flour into the burger mixture until combined. Then shape 4 patties out of rounded ½ cup (140 g) scoops, and place them on the baking sheet.

Bake the burgers for 10 minutes, then carefully flip them over, baking for another 10 minutes. While the burgers are baking, grill the pineapple and onions, following the instructions below. The burgers will be done when they are light brown on the top. Pull them out of the oven and brush with the remaining teriyaki sauce.

Grill the pineapple and red onion slices for 3 minutes on each side until they have softened and grill marks are visible.

To make the burgers, start with 4 bottom buns, then place 2 butter lettuce leaves on each, followed by a burger patty. Divide the grilled pineapple and onions among the burgers, and lastly, spread 1 tablespoon (15 g) of Garlic Mayo on the underside of each top bun. Top burger with bun and serve.

YIELD: 4 BURGERS

TIP: YOU CAN MAKE THESE PATTIES AHEAD OF TIME BY HAND-SHAPING THEM, STACKING THEM WITH WAXED PAPER IN BETWEEN, AND FREEZING THEM BEFORE YOU GET TO THE BAKING STAGE. MAKE SURE TO THAW THEM FULLY BEFORE BAKING.

BUTTERNUT MAC AND TREES

• UNDER 10 INGREDIENTS • 30 MINUTES OR LESS • ONE PAN
• GLUTEN FREE • SOY FREE • NUT FREE • OIL FREE • SUGAR FREE

My go-to dish for a last-minute dinner, especially if my boy-friend is eating, is a pot of vegan mac and cheese. While I've figured out many hacks when it comes to making a fast mac, I love this recipe because it includes so many vegetables, but only the broccoli is obvious. If you really want to make this a classic, slice up a couple veggie dogs and throw them in with the sauce!

2¼ cups (205 g) gluten-free pasta, such as elbows, fusilli, or shells

2 cups (160 g) broccoli florets

2 cups (475 ml) Butternut Cheese Sauce (page 196)

1½ tablespoons (15 g) soy-free vegan butter

¼ cup (60 ml) unsweetened nondairy milk

¼ teaspoon salt, to taste

Prepare the pasta according to the package instructions, but in the last 2 minutes of boiling add the broccoli florets to the pot. Once the pasta is cooked, strain the water from the pot. Return the pot to the stove over medium-low heat.

Add the Butternut Cheese Sauce, vegan butter, and nondairy milk to the pot, stirring frequently, until the butter is melted and the pasta is evenly coated. Season with salt to taste, and serve hot.

YIELD: 4 SERVINGS

TIP: WHEN IT COMES TO COOKING WITH GLUTEN-FREE NOODLES, I LOVE THE QUALITY OF BROWN RICE PASTA AS IT MOST CLOSELY RESEMBLES WHEAT PASTA. BUT, IF YOU'RE LOOKING FOR A LITTLE MORE PROTEIN IN YOUR MAC AND CHEESE, TRY USING LEGUME- OR QUINOA-BASED PASTAS.

TEMPEH ADOBO TOSTADAS

• 30 MINUTES OR LESS
• GLUTEN FREE • NUT FREE • SUGAR FREE

Even if you're the most dedicated follower of Taco Tuesday, you should definitely try out a Tostada Tuesday! It starts with a crunchy base, creamy beans, and seasoned tempeh, and it ends with crunchy cabbage and cooling salsa. Stack it with whatever else you see fit, because the sky is the limit.

FOR THE TEMPEH ADOBO:

1 tablespoon (15 ml) sunflower oil
8 ounces (225 g) tempeh, diced
½ cup (70 g) diced yellow onion
½ cup (75 g) diced green bell pepper
1 cup (235 ml) vegetable broth
¾ teaspoon paprika
½ teaspoon onion powder
½ teaspoon dried oregano
¼ teaspoon black pepper
¼ teaspoon ground cumin
⅛ teaspoon chipotle powder
¾ teaspoon salt

FOR THE TOSTADA:

3 tablespoons (45 ml) sunflower oil
4 corn tortillas, 6 inches (15 cm) in diameter
Pinch of salt
1 can (16 ounces, or 455 g) vegetarian refried beans
1 cup (75 g) shredded red cabbage
2 tablespoons (5 g) chopped fresh cilantro
½ cup (120 g) salsa

TO MAKE THE TEMPEH ADOBO:

In a skillet, warm the oil over medium-high heat. Once hot, add the tempeh, yellow onions, and bell peppers. Sauté for 3 minutes, or until the onions are mostly translucent and browning on the edges. Adjust the heat to medium, add the broth to the skillet, and simmer the tempeh mixture for 5 minutes, uncovered.

Add the paprika, onion powder, oregano, pepper, cumin, and chipotle powder to the skillet, stirring until combined. Sauté until all the liquid has evaporated, and season with salt. Take the skillet off the heat, but cover it with a lid to keep warm.

TO MAKE THE TOSTADA:

In a small pan, warm the oil over medium heat. To test the oil temperature, drop a small chunk of bread into it. If the bread sizzles, you are good to go.

Keep a plate lined with paper towels off to the side. Drop one tortilla in the oil and fry for 3 minutes, then flip and fry for another 3 minutes, or until bubbly and golden brown. Remove it from the oil, set it on a paper towel, and sprinkle with salt. Repeat the process for the remaining tortillas.

To assemble, divide the refried beans between the 4 tostadas, spreading them out to cover most of the surface. Next, divide the tempeh into fourths and top with some beans, then follow it with cabbage, cilantro, and salsa. Serve hot.

YIELD: 4 TOSTADAS

CAULIFLOWER ALFREDO WITH GRILLED ASPARAGUS

• UNDER 10 INGREDIENTS • 30 MINUTES OR LESS
• GLUTEN-FREE OPTION • SOY FREE • SUGAR FREE

Sometimes the title "vegan cook" can be synonymous with "magician" because we are over here hiding vegetables in everything we can! This creamy cauliflower sauce is wonderfully creamy and silky smooth. It pairs well with the grilled asparagus atop your perfect pile of pasta.

FOR THE CAULIFLOWER SAUCE:

3 cups (300 g) cauliflower florets

1 cup (135 g) chopped white onion

⅓ cup (45 g) raw pine nuts

3 cloves garlic, peeled

2 tablespoons (10 g) nutritional yeast

1 tablespoon (15 ml) lemon juice

1 teaspoon salt

½ teaspoon white pepper

FOR THE ASSEMBLY:

8 ounces (225 g) fettuccini pasta, gluten-free, if necessary

8 ounces (225 g) asparagus, woody ends trimmed

1 tablespoon (15 ml) sunflower oil

Pinch of salt

Pinch of black pepper

2 tablespoons (20 g) toasted pine nuts

TO MAKE THE CAULIFLOWER SAUCE:

Place the cauliflower, white onions, raw pine nuts, and garlic in a pot, then add water until mostly covered. Cover the pot and bring it to a boil over medium-high heat. Adjust the heat to medium and boil with the lid slightly vented for 10 to 12 minutes, or until the cauliflower is fork tender.

Carefully drain the pot, and place the boiled cauliflower, onions, pine nuts, and garlic in a blender, along with the nutritional yeast, lemon juice, salt, and pepper. Purée until completely smooth, and set aside.

TO ASSEMBLE:

Preheat a grill to 400°F (200°C). Prepare the pasta according to the package instructions. While that is cooking, place the asparagus in a bowl and coat with the oil, salt, and pepper. Grill the asparagus for 2 minutes on each side, or until grill marks are very prominent.

Once the pasta is cooked, drain the water, and pour the cauliflower sauce over the noodles. Cook, uncovered, over medium-low heat until the sauce has thickened slightly, roughly 3 minutes. Divide the pasta among 4 plates or shallow bowls, then top with grilled asparagus and toasted pine nuts. Serve.

YIELD: 4 SERVINGS

TIP: IF YOU WANT TO MAKE THIS DISH EVEN FANCIER, ADD A DRIZZLE OF TRUFFLE OIL OVER THE TOP OF EACH PLATE BEFORE SERVING.

HEARTY SKILLET CORNBREAD

- 30 MINUTES OR LESS
- GLUTEN FREE • NUT FREE

If you love cornbread as much as I do, you could probably make a meal out of it—much to your health teacher's chagrin. In this case, I'd prefer you do make a meal out of it! This Hearty Skillet Cornbread is filling, but also filled with vegetables, peppers, and seasoned soyrizo. For an even more well-rounded meal, serve yours on a bed of mixed greens.

FOR THE SOYRIZO MIX-INS:

1 cup (120 g) chopped zucchini
1 cup (255 g) soyrizo
1 cup (130 g) corn kernels
½ cup (150 g) diced roasted red pepper
½ cup (70 g) diced yellow onion

FOR THE CORNBREAD BATTER:

1 cup (160 g) cornmeal
1 cup (135 g) gluten-free all-purpose flour
2 tablespoons (15 g) ground flaxseed
1½ teaspoons salt
1 teaspoon baking powder
1 cup (235 ml) unsweetened nondairy milk
6 tablespoons (90 ml) melted coconut oil
⅓ cup (80 ml) water
¼ cup (60 ml) agave nectar
2 tablespoons (5 g) chopped fresh cilantro

TO MAKE THE SOYRIZO MIX-INS:

First, preheat the oven to 375°F (190°C, or gas mark 5). Warm an 8-inch (20 cm) cast-iron skillet over medium-high heat, and add the zucchini, soyrizo, corn, red pepper, and yellow onions. Sauté for 5 minutes, stirring occasionally.

TO MAKE THE CORNBREAD BATTER:

In a large mixing bowl, whisk together the cornmeal, flour, flaxseed, salt, and baking powder until evenly combined. Make a well in the middle of the dry ingredients and pour in the nondairy milk, coconut oil, water, and agave nectar. Fold the batter together until well mixed, with no dry spots.

Next, take the skillet off the heat and pour the batter over the sautéed mix-ins. Fold together a few times, then place the skillet in the oven and bake for 20 minutes, or until an inserted toothpick draws clean. Cool the skillet on a rack for 5 to 10 minutes before cutting into it; sprinkle cilantro over the top and serve.

YIELD: 4 SERVINGS

TIP: THIS SKILLET CORNBREAD IS ESPECIALLY TASTY WHEN SERVED WITH A PAT OF VEGAN BUTTER ON TOP!

BUCKWHEAT-STUFFED ACORN SQUASH

• 30 MINUTES OR LESS • PORTABLE • MAKE AHEAD
• GLUTEN FREE • SOY FREE • NUT FREE

You know fall has hit when the markets have out their massive displays of fall and winter squash. It's one of my favorite things about the seasons changing. And while I've made many a stuffed squash, I'm obsessed with this version. It has the perfect balance of sweet and savory, with cooked grains, tart cranberries, chopped greens, and maple tahini sauce.

FOR THE SQUASH:
2 small acorn squash, halved, seeds scooped
Cooking oil spray
¼ teaspoon salt
¼ teaspoon black pepper

FOR THE FILLING:
1 cup (235 ml) vegetable broth
½ cup (70 g) diced sweet onion
½ cup (85 g) buckwheat groats
1 cup (100 g) thinly sliced Brussels sprouts
½ cup (35 g) chopped radicchio
¼ cup (25 g) dried cranberries
1 teaspoon fresh rosemary, minced
⅛ teaspoon black pepper
¼ cup (16 g) roasted pepitas (shelled pumpkin seeds)

FOR THE DRESSING:
⅓ cup (85 g) tahini
¼ cup (60 ml) water
1 tablespoon (15 ml) orange juice
1 tablespoon (15 ml) maple syrup
¼ teaspoon garlic powder
⅛ teaspoon salt, or to taste

TO MAKE THE SQUASH:
Preheat the oven to 400°F (200°C, or gas mark 6), and fill a large baking dish with a thin layer of water. Place the squash halves in the dish cut-side up, and poke a few holes in each one with a fork. Lightly coat them with cooking oil spray, then sprinkle salt and pepper over the tops. Bake for 25 minutes, or until fork tender.

TO MAKE THE FILLING:
While the squash is baking, place the vegetable broth and onions in a saucepan, bringing it to a simmer over medium heat. Cook for 3 to 5 minutes, or until the onions are nearly translucent. Add the buckwheat groats to the pan. Adjust the heat to medium-low, cover with a lid, and simmer for 10 minutes.

Once the groats are tender, fold the Brussels, radicchio, cranberries, rosemary, and black pepper into the mixture. Cook until the the radicchio reduces in size, about 2 minutes. Turn the heat off, leaving the mixture covered to keep warm.

TO MAKE THE DRESSING:
In a small bowl, whisk the tahini, water, orange juice, maple syrup, garlic powder, and salt together until smooth. Taste and add more seasonings per your preference.

TO ASSEMBLE:
Once the squash halves are baked, stuff each one with some buckwheat mixture, then drizzle the tahini sauce on top, and sprinkle pepitas over them. Serve hot.

YIELD: 4 SERVINGS

ROASTED VEGGIE QUINOA BOWL

• UNDER 10 INGREDIENTS • 30 MINUTES OR LESS • MAKE AHEAD
• GLUTEN FREE • SOY FREE • SUGAR FREE

Some evenings, when dinnertime comes around after a busy day, all I want is a super simple dinner of grains and vegetables. This roasted veggie bowl fits the bill, but it is still a few steps above just steaming some broccoli and rice and calling it a day. The addition of crunchy pistachios and tart lemon juice are really the best finishing touches to this dish.

FOR THE ROASTED VEGETABLES:

1 pound (455 g) fingerling potatoes, quartered

½ pound (225 g) whole green beans, ends trimmed

2 cups (200 g) wedged green cabbage

1 cup (120 g) halved shallots

¼ cup (10 g) chopped fresh dill

2 tablespoons (30 ml) olive oil

½ teaspoon salt

¼ teaspoon black pepper

FOR THE QUINOA:

2⅔ cups (635 ml) vegetable broth

1⅓ cups (250 g) tri-colored quinoa

FOR THE ASSEMBLY:

½ cup (60 g) chopped roasted pistachios

2 tablespoons (30 ml) lemon juice

⅛ teaspoon salt

⅛ teaspoon black pepper

TO MAKE THE ROASTED VEGETABLES:

Preheat the oven to 400°F (200°C, or gas mark 6) and get out a large baking sheet. Lay the potatoes, green beans, cabbage, and shallots out on the baking sheet. Scatter the dill over them. Drizzle with oil, and sprinkle with salt and pepper. Toss gently until everything is coated evenly, and roast for 10 minutes. Stir the vegetables around, then roast for another 10 minutes. Turn the oven off and vent the door, but leave the sheet inside to keep the vegetables warm.

TO MAKE THE QUINOA:

While the veggies are roasting, place the vegetable broth and quinoa in a medium-sized pan, cover, and bring to a simmer over medium heat. Adjust the heat to medium-low and simmer for 18 to 20 minutes, then fluff with a spoon or fork.

TO ASSEMBLE:

Divide the roasted vegetables and quinoa between 4 bowls, then top each with 2 tablespoons (15 g) of pistachios, ½ tablespoon of lemon juice, and a pinch of salt and pepper. Serve warm.

YIELD: 4 SERVINGS

PARTY NACHO PLATTER

• 30 MINUTES OR LESS • ONE PAN
• GLUTEN FREE • SOY FREE • NUT-FREE OPTION • OIL FREE • SUGAR FREE

It may sound a little weird, but one of my parents' favorite easy dinners is a huge plate of nachos to share. Typically, you would order nachos as an appetizer off the menu, but I think we all know full well that it's a main course on its own. Whip up a platter of these impressive nachos for friends and family, and dare them to ask for seconds!

FOR THE QUESO:

2 cups (475 ml) Butternut Cheese Sauce (page 196)

¼ cup (20 g) nutritional yeast

½ teaspoon ground cumin

1 tablespoon (15 g) pickled jalapeños

1 can (15 ounces, or 425 g) pinto beans, drained and rinsed

FOR THE ASSEMBLY:

10 ounces (280 g) corn tortilla chips

2 cups (350 g) Buckwheat Taco Meat (page 185), warmed

1 cup (40 g) packed shredded romaine

1 cup (200 g) diced tomatoes

¼ cup (35 g) thinly sliced avocado

¼ cup (35 g) thinly sliced radishes

2 tablespoons (30 g) Simple Cashew Cream (page 186) or vegan sour cream, nut free if necessary

1 tablespoon (3 g) minced fresh cilantro

TO MAKE THE QUESO:

In a small pot over medium heat, whisk the Butternut Cheese Sauce, nutritional yeast, cumin, and pickled jalapeños together until combined. Bring to a simmer, then adjust the heat to medium-low, and add the pinto beans. Simmer for 5 minutes, stirring occasionally.

TO ASSEMBLE:

Spread the chips out on a large platter, then cover them with the queso-bean mixture, followed by the Buckwheat Taco Meat, romaine, tomatoes, avocado, radishes, dollops of Simple Cashew Cream, and lastly, minced cilantro. Serve warm.

YIELD: 4 TO 6 SERVINGS

TIP: TO SAVE EVEN MORE TIME, YOU CAN BUY PREMADE VEGAN BEEF CRUMBLES TO USE INSTEAD OF THE BUCKWHEAT TACO MEAT, AND STORE-BOUGHT VEGAN SOUR CREAM INSTEAD OF THE CASHEW CREAM!

PRESSURE COOKER PESTO SPAGHETTI SQUASH

• UNDER 10 INGREDIENTS • 30 MINUTES OR LESS • MAKE AHEAD • ONE PAN
• GLUTEN FREE • SOY-FREE OPTION • NUT FREE • SUGAR FREE

If you've never had spaghetti squash, and are hesitant to try it because of the hype, hesitate no more. Instead of waiting 45+ minutes for your squash to cook, a pressure cooker cuts the time spent wondering if you'll like it considerably. Trust me, you will love this recipe, where the squash is paired with a nut-free pesto and crunchy pepitas.

3-pound (1360 g) spaghetti squash

1 cup water

1½ cups (360 g) Nut-Free Pepita Pesto (page 198)

½ teaspoon salt

¼ teaspoon black pepper

¾ cup (90 g) roasted, salted pepitas (shelled pumpkin seeds)

¼ cup (25 g) Sunflower Parmesan (page 193; optional)

Cut the spaghetti squash in half, through its cross section, instead of lengthwise. This will give you longer "noodles." Pour the water into a large pressure cooker, and insert a wire rack or steam basket. Poke a few holes in each squash half, then place them in the pressure cooker. Seal the top and bring up to high pressure, cooking the squash for 7 minutes once pressure is reached.

After 7 minutes, take the pressure cooker off the stove, and vent the steam until there is no longer pressure inside. Remove the top and allow the squash to cool until you can safely hold it in your hands. Once this is possible, drain the water from the pot, and remove the rack.

Using a fork, scrape the squash out of its skin and back into the pot. Discard the skin. Add the Nut-Free Pepita Pesto, salt, and pepper to the squash. Fold until well coated. Divide the mixture between 4 bowls, and top each with pepitas and optional Sunflower Parmesan. Serve hot.

YIELD: 4 SERVINGS

TIP: THIS DISH IS THE GREENEST OF THE GREEN, SO IF YOU WANT TO CREATE LITTLE POPS OF COLOR, ADD SOME HALVED CHERRY TOMATOES TO THE MIX!

COCONUT CURRY SWEET POTATO NOODLES

Would this really be a vegan cookbook without some form of spiralized veggie noodles? I think not! Here's a fun and less traditional way to incorporate sweet potatoes into your curry. I love making this dish when I'm feeling a little under the weather, when the ginger and spice can help put some pep in my step.

1 teaspoon coconut oil

1 cup (140 g) diced yellow onion

1 cup (130 g) diced red bell pepper

1 large carrot, peeled and sliced

1 tablespoon (15 g) sliced jalapeño

1½ teaspoons minced ginger

2 cups (330 g) canned chickpeas, drained and rinsed

1 tablespoon (5 g) yellow curry powder

1½ cups (355 ml) vegetable broth

1 can (13.5 ounces, or 400 ml) lite coconut milk

4 cups (300 g) spiralized sweet potato

2 cups (70 g) baby spinach

¼ cup (10 g) chopped fresh cilantro, divided

1 teaspoon salt, or to taste

1 tablespoon (15 ml) lime juice

Warm the coconut oil in a large pot over medium heat. Once hot, add the yellow onions, bell peppers, carrots, jalapeño, and ginger. Sauté for 7 minutes, or until the onions are translucent and the carrots are tender. Stir the chickpeas and curry powder into the sautéed mixture until everything is well coated in curry powder.

Add the broth and coconut milk to the pot, and simmer for 5 minutes. Lastly, add the sweet potato noodles, spinach, and 2 tablespoons (5 g) of cilantro to the pot. Simmer for an additional 5 minutes, stirring occasionally. Test the sweet potato noodles to see if they are "al dente," then stir the salt and lime juice into the curry.

Divide the curry between 4 bowls, and garnish each with the remaining cilantro before serving.

YIELD: 4 SERVINGS

NOTE: FOR A RICHER CURRY, USE FULL-FAT COCONUT MILK IN PLACE OF THE LITE COCONUT MILK.

SAVORY PUFF PASTRY TARTLETS

- PORTABLE
- NUT FREE • SUGAR FREE

If you want to make a seemingly fancy main course without it
actually taking much work, these tartlets are for you! Not only do
they taste delicious, their single-serving size makes them cuter,
and they take less time to bake.

FOR THE TARTLETS:

12.3 ounces (350 g) silken tofu

2 tablespoons (10 g) nutritional yeast

1 teaspoon cornstarch

1 teaspoon lemon juice

1 clove garlic, peeled

1 tablespoon (5 g) fresh basil

¾ teaspoon salt

1 sheet (245 g) thawed vegan puff pastry

1 cup (170 g) tomato slices

1 cup (120 g) zucchini slices

Cooking oil spray

FOR THE GARNISH:

¼ cup (60 ml) balsamic vinegar

¼ teaspoon coarse salt

4 basil leaves

NOTE: IF YOU DON'T HAVE THE PANS TO MAKE
THESE SINGLE-SERVING SIZE, USE A 9-INCH
(23-CM) TART OR PIE PAN AND ASSEMBLE
AS ONE TART. BAKE FOR 35 TO 40 MINUTES,
THOUGH BAKING TIMES MAY VARY.

Preheat the oven to 400°F (200°C, or gas mark 6), and get
out four 4-inch (10 cm) tartlet pans and a baking sheet.

Place the silken tofu, nutritional yeast, cornstarch, lemon
juice, garlic, basil, and salt in a blender, puréeing until
completely smooth. Set aside.

Roll the puff pastry sheet out until it is roughly 10 x 10 inches
(25 x 25 cm), and cut it into 4 equal squares. Lay each square
over a tartlet dish, pressing in lightly to fit the bottom and
walls. Pour a heaping ⅓ cup (75 g) of filling into each crust,
then layer tomato and zucchini slices on the filling, and spray
a light coat of cooking oil on top.

Place the tartlet pans on the baking sheet. Bake for 18 to 20
minutes, or until the corners of the puff pastry are golden
brown. The filling will be slightly soft and creamy.

TO MAKE THE GARNISH:

While the tartlets are baking, bring the balsamic vinegar to a
simmer in a small saucepan over medium-low heat. Simmer
for 5 to 7 minutes, or until it has reduced by half, then remove
from the heat.

Once the tartlets are done, garnish each with a drizzle of
balsamic reduction, a pinch of coarse salt, and 1 basil leaf.
Serve warm.

YIELD: 4 SERVINGS

SPICY JACKFRUIT CHILI

• 30 MINUTES OR LESS • MAKE AHEAD • ONE PAN
• GLUTEN FREE • SOY FREE • NUT FREE • SUGAR FREE

I agree that to get the absolute best chili, you'll need a couple hours to let it stew and enhance all of the flavors. But I shocked a few people with this chili, which only took me 30 minutes! So, make a batch of this chili when you're short on comfort and time—without missing any of that bold flavor.

1 tablespoon (15 ml) sunflower oil

2 cans (40 ounces, or 1135 g) green jackfruit in brine, drained and rinsed with seeds removed

1 cup (140 g) diced yellow onion

1 red bell pepper, seeded and diced

1 tablespoon (15 g) minced jalapeño

2 tablespoons (35 g) tomato paste

1 can (15 ounces, or 425 g) black beans, drained and rinsed

1½ cups (375 ml) vegetable broth

1 cup (170 g) chopped tomatoes

2 teaspoons (10 ml) apple cider vinegar

1½ teaspoons chili powder

¼ teaspoon chipotle powder

½ teaspoon smoked paprika

1 teaspoon ground coriander

1 teaspoon salt, or to taste

¼ cup (12 g) diced scallions

¼ cup (30 g) vegan cheese crumbles or shreds (optional)

Warm the oil in a large pot over medium-high heat. Once hot, add the jackfruit and yellow onions, sautéing them for 3 minutes to brown the edges. Adjust the heat to medium, and add the bell peppers, jalapeño, and tomato paste to the pot. Sauté the mixture for 5 minutes, or until the peppers have softened and the onions are translucent. While doing so, break the jackfruit up into smaller pieces.

Next, add the black beans, vegetable broth, chopped tomatoes, apple cider vinegar, chili powder, chipotle powder, smoked paprika, and coriander to the pot. Bring the mixture to a boil. Adjust the heat to medium-low and simmer, covered, for 10 minutes, stirring occasionally.

After the chili has simmered, season with salt to taste. Divide the chili between 4 bowls, topping each with 1 tablespoon (3 g) of scallions and 1 tablespoon (7 g) of optional vegan cheese. Serve hot.

YIELD: 4 SERVINGS

TIP: GREEN OR YOUNG JACKFRUIT IN BRINE CAN BE FOUND AT MOST ASIAN MARKETS, PLUS SOME NATURAL FOOD STORES. MAKE SURE TO REMOVE THE SEEDS HIDDEN IN ITS FLESH, AS THEY CAN BECOME HARD AND UNPLEASANT DURING THE COOKING PROCESS.

PORTOBELLO FAJITA SALAD

• 30 MINUTES OR LESS • PORTABLE • MAKE AHEAD
• GLUTEN FREE • SOY FREE • NUT FREE

There is a restaurant that I used to frequent regularly with family that had really good fajita dishes, served with a magical green sauce and fluffy cornbread-like balls on the side. While I don't find myself there anymore, this fajita salad is even better than the dish I remember!

FOR THE AVOCADO DRESSING:

½ cup (120 g) mashed avocado

¾ cup (175 ml) water

¼ cup (60 ml) lime juice

2 tablespoons (30 ml) olive oil

2 teaspoons (10 ml) agave nectar

1 clove garlic, peeled

¼ teaspoon salt

½ cup (10 g) fresh cilantro

FOR THE FAJITA SALAD:

1½ tablespoons (25 ml) sunflower oil

1 cup (120 g) slivered red onion

1 sliced poblano pepper

1 cup (100 g) sliced bell pepper (mixed colors)

2 tablespoons (15 g) sliced jalapeño

8 ounces (225 g) sliced portobello mushrooms

½ teaspoon salt

⅛ teaspoon black pepper

8 ounces (225 g) romaine lettuce, chopped

1 can (15 ounces, or 425 g) black beans, drained and rinsed

¼ cup (10 g) dried sweet corn (optional)

TO MAKE THE DRESSING:

Place the avocado, water, lime juice, olive oil, agave nectar, garlic, and salt in a blender. Purée until completely smooth. Add the cilantro and pulse until the leaves are broken up into smaller pieces. Transfer the dressing to a squeeze bottle or jar, and refrigerate.

TO MAKE THE FAJITA SALAD:

In a large pan, warm the oil over medium-high heat. Once hot, add the red onions, poblano pepper, bell peppers, and jalapeño to the pan. Sauté for 5 to 7 minutes, browning the pepper mix on a couple sides and stirring occasionally. Once the onions are nearly translucent, add the mushrooms to the pan. Continue to sauté for 5 minutes, or until the mushrooms have decreased in size and are browned on the edges. Season with salt and pepper.

Divide the lettuce between 4 plates, then top with black beans and fajita veggies. Drizzle dressing over the salad, or serve it on the side. Garnish with the optional dried sweet corn, and serve.

YIELD: 4 SERVINGS

TIP: YOU CAN MAKE THIS SALAD AHEAD OF TIME, WITH THE DRESSING ON THE SIDE, AND CHILL THE FAJITA VEGGIES, AS THEY STILL TASTE GREAT COLD.

PITA PIZZA TRIO

• UNDER 10 INGREDIENTS • 30 MINUTES OR LESS • ONE PAN
• SOY FREE • NUT-FREE OPTION • OIL FREE

Pizza is the food of peace, in my opinion. I've been hard-pressed to find someone that doesn't like it, and it is certainly a great option for feeding multiple people. Instead of making your own crust, start with a simple pita and build up from there for your own pizza party in minutes!

FOR THE PIZZA BASE:

4 pitas

1 cup (245 g) Chunky Tomato Sauce (page 199)

FOR PINEAPPLE BACON PIZZAS:

1 cup (115 g) vegan mozzarella shreds

½ cup (85 g) pineapple chunks

¼ cup (20 g) Coconut Bacon (page 195)

¼ cup (30 g) sliced black olives

FOR SIMPLE VEGGIE PIZZAS:

½ cup (20 g) packed baby spinach

½ cup (50 g) quartered artichoke hearts

½ cup (35 g) sliced baby bella mushrooms

¼ cup (30 g) thinly sliced red onion

2 tablespoons (20 g) raw pine nuts

¼ teaspoon dried oregano

FOR CAPRESE PIZZAS:

¼ cup (60 g) Simple Cashew Cream (page 199)

½ tablespoon (2.5 g) nutritional yeast

¼ teaspoon garlic powder

½ cup (100 g) tomato slices

¼ cup (10 g) fresh basil leaves

1 clove garlic, minced

¼ teaspoon coarse salt

⅛ teaspoon cracked pepper

TO MAKE THE PIZZA BASE:

Preheat the oven to 400°F (200°C, or gas mark 6), with a large pizza stone inside. Or have a large baking sheet handy. Lay out 4 pitas, and spread ¼ cup (60 g) Chunky Tomato Sauce over each one. Top the pizzas with any of the three options below, or customize your own!

TO MAKE PINEAPPLE BACON PIZZAS:

Sprinkle cheese shreds over the sauce, then top with pineapple, Coconut Bacon, and black olive slices. Place in the oven for 10 to 12 minutes, or until the cheese has melted.

TO MAKE SIMPLE VEGGIE PIZZAS:

Divide the spinach, artichoke hearts, mushrooms, and red onions between the 4 pitas, then top with pine nuts and dried oregano. Bake for 10 to 12 minutes, or until the pitas are golden around the edges.

TO MAKE CAPRESE PIZZAS:

In a small bowl, stir together the Simple Cashew Cream, nutritional yeast, and garlic powder. Then top each pita with 1 tablespoon (15 g) of the Simple Cashew Cream mixture, followed by tomato slices, basil, garlic, salt, and pepper. Bake for 10 to 12 minutes, or until the pitas are golden around the edges.

YIELD: 4 PIZZAS

NOTE: EACH OF THE TOPPING OPTIONS MAKES ENOUGH FOR ALL FOUR PITA PIZZAS.

CHAPTER 6

BULK COOKING

MEALS THAT MAKE UPSCALING RECIPES A BREEZE

Whether you are cooking for a crowd or meal prepping for a week's worth of lunches and dinners, bulk cooking will cover your bases. These recipes can easily be doubled or tripled for many servings of a well-rounded meal.

WINTER ROOT TEMPEH BAKE

While a lot of fall and winter foods end up being predominately beige, orange, or brown, this Winter Root Tempeh Bake has some stunning colors. Here, we use beautiful beets, as well as their delicious greens, for a hearty, simple meal. The orange-maple glaze really creates a pop of flavor, too!

12 ounces (340 g) chopped tempeh

1 cup (235 ml) vegetable broth

2 cups (285 g) chopped beets, with greens separated

1½ cups (200 g) chopped carrots

1½ cups (210 g) chopped celery root

1 cup (145 g) chopped parsnips

1 cup (130 g) chopped turnips

2 tablespoons (30 ml) orange juice

2 tablespoons (30 ml) olive oil

2 tablespoons (30 ml) maple syrup

1 teaspoon dried sage

1 teaspoon dried thyme

1 teaspoon orange zest

¾ teaspoon salt

½ teaspoon black pepper

2 cups (360 g) chopped beet greens or mixed greens

4 orange wedges

Preheat the oven to 400°F (200°C, or gas mark 6), and have ready a large baking dish.

In a medium pan, place the tempeh and vegetable broth, bringing it to a boil over medium heat. Reduce the heat to medium-low and simmer for 10 minutes.

Transfer the tempeh to the large baking dish (reserve the vegetable broth). Add the beets, carrots, celery root, parsnips, and turnips. Drizzle orange juice, olive oil, and maple syrup over the top, then sprinkle with sage, thyme, orange zest, salt, and pepper. Toss the vegetable mix until evenly coated, then pour the reserved vegetable broth from the tempeh pan into the baking dish.

Bake for 20 minutes, stir the mixture, and bake for an additional 30 minutes, or until the root veggies are fork tender and starting to brown on the edges. Take out of the oven, and sprinkle with a pinch of salt and pepper.

Divide the greens between 4 plates, then top with the winter root tempeh bake and 1 orange wedge per plate.

YIELD: 4 SERVINGS

NOTE: IF THE ORANGE SQUEEZE ISN'T ENOUGH FOR YOU, DRIZZLE SOME OF THE DRESSING FROM PAGE 110 OVER THE TOP OF EACH PLATE.

DROP BISCUIT POT PIE

• MAKE AHEAD
• SOY FREE • NUT FREE • SUGAR FREE

If you have my first book, *Vegan Bowl Attack!*, you know that I love my biscuits. Here, I've modified them a little bit to be the perfect topping for this white bean pot pie. Buttery, fluffy, warm, and creamy. Are you drooling yet?

FOR THE FILLING:

1 tablespoon (15 ml) sunflower oil

1 cup (140 g) diced white onion

1 cup (100 g) diced celery

2 carrots, diced

3 cups (270 g) sliced baby bella mushrooms

1 cup (40 g) chopped kale or other hearty green

1 can (15 ounces, or 425 g) white beans, including their liquid

2 tablespoons (20 g) unbleached all-purpose flour

½ teaspoon dried sage

½ teaspoon dried thyme

¼ teaspoon dried oregano

¼ teaspoon white pepper

1 cup (235 ml) vegetable broth

½ teaspoon salt, or to taste

FOR THE DROP BISCUITS:

¾ cup (100 g) unbleached all-purpose flour

½ cup (65 g) whole wheat pastry flour

1½ teaspoons baking powder

¾ teaspoon salt

¼ teaspoon black pepper

⅓ cup (60 g) vegetable shortening or cold vegan butter

½ cup (120 ml) unsweetened nondairy milk

TO MAKE THE FILLING:

Warm the oil in a large pan over medium heat. Once hot, add the white onions, celery, and carrots to the pan. Sauté for 5 to 7 minutes, or until the onions are translucent. Add the mushrooms and kale to the pan, cooking for 3 minutes.

Next, stir the white beans and their liquid, flour, sage, thyme, oregano, and white pepper into the vegetables until evenly combined. Pour the vegetable broth into the pan and bring to a simmer, then adjust the heat to medium-low. Simmer for 2 minutes, add salt to taste, and set aside.

TO MAKE THE DROP BISCUITS:

Preheat the oven to 425ºF (220ºC, or gas mark 7), and have ready a 6 x 10-inch (15 x 25 cm) or 8 x 8-inch (20 x 20 cm) baking dish.

In a large mixing bowl, sift together the all-purpose flour, pastry flour, baking powder, salt, and black pepper. Add the vegetable shortening to the dry mixture, and cut it into the flour with a fork or pastry cutter until it resembles small pebbles. Add the nondairy milk to the bowl, and mix until there are no dry spots.

Transfer the filling to the baking dish, and place scoops of drop biscuit dough over the top in a single layer. Bake the pot pie for 30 minutes, or until the tops of the biscuits are golden. Cool on a rack for 5 to 10 minutes before serving.

YIELD: 4 SERVINGS

TIP: TO MAKE THIS FOR A LARGER CROWD, DOUBLE THIS RECIPE TO FIT A LARGER BAKING DISH, OR QUADRUPLE IT TO FIT TWO OF THEM! FOR THE LARGER SIZE, BAKE FOR 40 TO 45 MINUTES.

CHICKPEA TENDIES & WAFFLES

• MAKE AHEAD
• SOY FREE • NUT FREE

Now, if you've never heard of chick'n and waffles, I assure you, it's an awesome combination. The first time I had it was in my pre-vegan days, and now I've enjoyed several vegan versions that were even better! While I love fried foods, I baked these chickpea tendies to keep them on the healthier side. Slather this duo in the spicy syrup and enjoy!

FOR THE CHICKPEA TENDIES:

2 cans (30 ounces, or 850 g) chickpeas, drained, 2 tablespoons (30 ml) aquafaba (a.k.a. chickpea brine) reserved

½ cup (70 g) diced yellow onion

2 teaspoons (5 g) salt-free poultry seasoning

1 teaspoon salt

1 teaspoon garlic powder

¼ teaspoon black pepper

½ teaspoon paprika

½ cup (60 g) vital wheat gluten

⅓ cup (30 g) panko bread crumbs

3 tablespoons (25 g) sesame seeds

1 teaspoon onion powder

FOR THE WAFFLES:

1¼ cups (295 ml) unsweetened nondairy milk

2 tablespoons (30 ml) lemon juice

1 tablespoon (15 g) sunflower oil

1 teaspoon vanilla extract

1 cup (130 g) unbleached all-purpose flour

½ cup (55 g) quick-cooking oats

2 tablespoons (25 g) sugar

2 teaspoons (9 g) baking powder

Pinch of salt

FOR THE SPICY SYRUP:

⅓ cup (80 ml) maple syrup

1½ tablespoons (22.5 ml) hot sauce

TO MAKE THE CHICKPEA TENDIES:

Preheat the oven to 400°F (200°C, or gas mark 6), and line a baking sheet with parchment paper or a silicone baking mat.

Place the chickpeas with reserved aquafaba, yellow onions, poultry seasoning, salt, garlic powder, pepper, and paprika in a food processor equipped with an S-blade. Pulse the mixture until the chickpeas are broken up to about one-quarter of their original size. Sprinkle the vital wheat gluten over the chickpea "dough," and pulse a few times to evenly combine.

In a small bowl or plate with high edges, mix the panko crumbs, sesame seeds, and onion powder together. Lightly wet your hand with water, and form "cutlets" or "tender" shapes from 3-tablespoon-sized (45 g) scoops of the chickpea mixture. Gently press each tendie into the panko mixture until coated, then transfer to the baking sheet. Repeat until there are 12 chickpea tendies.

Bake for 12 minutes, then flip over, and bake an additional 12 minutes, or until they start to turn golden. While those are baking, start on the waffles.

TO MAKE THE WAFFLES:

Preheat a standard waffle maker (not a Belgian waffle maker), and have ready a blender. Place the nondairy milk, lemon juice, oil, vanilla, flour, oats, sugar, baking powder, and salt in the blender pitcher, in that order. Purée until smooth.

Allow the waffle batter to sit for 5 minutes to thicken, then pour it into your waffle maker. Cook the waffle for about 8 minutes, checking to see if it is ready once most of the steaming has stopped. Repeat until the waffle batter is used up.

TO MAKE THE SPICY SYRUP:

In a small bowl or jar, whisk the maple syrup and hot sauce together until combined.

TO SERVE:

Divide the waffles between 4 plates, and top each with 3 chickpea tendies. Serve hot with the spicy syrup on the side.

YIELD: 4 SERVINGS

TIP: YOU CAN MAKE BOTH THE CHICKPEA TENDIES AND WAFFLES AHEAD OF TIME. STORE THEM IN SEPARATE FREEZER-FRIENDLY BAGS OR CONTAINERS UNTIL YOU ARE READY TO REHEAT THEM AND SERVE!

SMOKY GREENS WITH RED BEANS AND GRITS

• 30 MINUTES OR LESS
• SOY FREE • NUT FREE

I must say, eating grits was not something I did while I was growing up, even though my mother was raised on them. We predominantly ate oats in the morning, but once I got into grits as an adult it was game over! I love that you can go sweet or savory with them. And in this case, it's super savory with slightly cheesy grits, smoky greens, and spicy beans. This dish is like a hug in a bowl!

FOR THE POLENTA GRITS:

3 cups (720 ml) vegetable broth
1 cup (140 g) polenta grits
¼ cup (20 g) nutritional yeast
¼ teaspoon black pepper
⅛ teaspoon salt, or to taste

FOR THE SMOKY GREENS:

1½ tablespoons (25 ml) sunflower oil
½ cup (45 g) diced shallots
8 ounces (225 g) cubed seitan
4 cups (200 g) packed chopped hearty greens, stems removed
1 can (15 ounces, or 425 g) red beans, drained and rinsed
1 tablespoon (15 ml) maple syrup
1 teaspoon apple cider vinegar
1 teaspoon liquid smoke
¼ teaspoon smoked paprika
⅛ teaspoon cayenne pepper
½ teaspoon salt, or to taste

TO MAKE THE POLENTA GRITS:

Place the vegetable broth, polenta grits, nutritional yeast, and pepper in a pot. Cover with a lid, and bring the mixture to a boil over medium heat. Stir, and adjust the heat to medium-low and simmer the grits for 18 to 20 minutes, stirring every 5 minutes. While the polenta is cooking, start on the smoky greens.

TO MAKE THE SMOKY GREENS:

Warm the oil in a large pan over medium heat. Once hot, add the shallots and seitan, and sauté for 2 minutes. Next, add the greens, red beans, maple syrup, apple cider vinegar, liquid smoke, paprika, and cayenne. Adjust the heat to medium-low, cover the pan, and cook for 10 minutes, stirring occasionally.

Once the greens are mostly wilted, without being mushy, season with salt to taste. Divide the polenta between 4 bowls. Top each with the smoky greens mixture, add salt to taste, and serve.

YIELD: 4 SERVINGS

TIP: THIS RECIPE IS GREAT TO DOUBLE FOR A FAMILY MEAL OR MEAL PREP, AS ALL YOU NEED ARE MORE INGREDIENTS AND LARGE POTS! COOKING TIMES ONLY INCREASE BY A MINUTE OR TWO IN THE EXPANSION OF THIS RECIPE.

BAKED BALSAMIC TOFU OVER MIXED GREENS

• UNDER 10 INGREDIENTS • MAKE AHEAD • PORTABLE
• GLUTEN FREE • NUT FREE • SUGAR FREE

When I first went vegan, balsamic-baked tofu was my jam!
Then, I got distracted with making a million versions of vegan
mac and cheese. So, with this recipe, I'm returning to my
vegan roots, which are simple but delicious. I love eating this
dish for lunch as it is filling, but not too heavy.

14 ounces (395 g) extra-firm tofu, drained
   and pressed (Save the container.)
¼ cup (60 ml) balsamic vinegar
2 tablespoons (30 ml) water
1 tablespoon (15 ml) olive oil
1 tablespoon (15 g) tomato paste
2 teaspoons (10 ml) Dijon mustard
½ teaspoon dried basil
½ teaspoon salt
¼ teaspoon black pepper
2⅔ cups (635 ml) vegetable broth
1⅓ cups (250 g) white quinoa
4 cups (160 g) mixed greens
1 cup (100 g) shredded carrots

In the empty tofu container, whisk together the balsamic
vinegar, water, olive oil, tomato paste, mustard, basil, salt,
and pepper. Cut the tofu block into 8 equal rectangles, and
place them in the tofu container with the marinade. Leave in
the refrigerator to marinate for 4 to 8 hours.

Preheat the oven to 400°F (200°C, or gas mark 6), and line a
baking sheet with parchment paper. Place the tofu pieces on
the parchment and drizzle the excess marinade over them.
Bake for 15 minutes, flip over, and bake for 15 more minutes.

While the tofu is baking, place the vegetable broth and quinoa
in a medium-sized pan, cover, and bring to a simmer over
medium heat. Adjust the heat to medium-low and simmer
for 18 to 20 minutes, then fluff with a spoon or fork.

Once both are done cooking, divide the mixed greens and
carrots between 4 bowls or containers, along with the quinoa
and tofu. Serve while the tofu is warm, or chill the dish and
eat it cold.

YIELD: 4 SERVINGS

TIP: IF YOU'VE NEVER PRESSED TOFU
BEFORE, DON'T WORRY—IT'S EASY! WRAP
YOUR BLOCK OF TOFU IN A CLEAN KITCHEN
TOWEL OR A FEW LAYERS OF PAPER
TOWELS, PLACE IT ON A FLAT PLATE, AND
PUT A CUTTING BOARD ON TOP OF IT. PLACE
HEAVY, STABLE ITEMS—LIKE COOKBOOKS—
ON THE CUTTING BOARD, AND LET IT SIT
FOR 20 TO 30 MINUTES TO SQUEEZE SOME
OF THE LIQUID OUT. YOU CAN ALSO BUY
A TOFU PRESS ONLINE TO MAKE IT MORE
CONVENIENT!

CREAMY MUSHROOM TEMPEH AND BROCCOLI

• MAKE AHEAD • PORTABLE
• GLUTEN-FREE OPTION • NUT FREE • SUGAR FREE

If you're looking for some stick-to-your-ribs goodness, this recipe is perfect! There's the gravy-like Creamy Mushroom Tempeh that seems more indulgent than it is; then you have the steamed broccoli and rice to keep it simple and balanced. I love a lot of black pepper in my gravy, and this recipe is no different, so adjust it according to your taste bud preferences.

FOR THE CREAMY MUSHROOM TEMPEH:

2 teaspoons (10 ml) sunflower oil

1 cup (140 g) diced yellow onion

2 cups (125 g) sliced baby bella mushrooms

8 ounces (225 g) tempeh, chopped

2 cups (475 ml) vegan beef broth or vegetable broth, divided

⅓ cup (45 g) all-purpose flour, gluten-free if necessary

1 cup (235 ml) unsweetened nondairy milk

1 teaspoon onion powder

½ to ¾ teaspoon black pepper

½ teaspoon ground sage

½ teaspoon salt, or to taste

FOR THE BROCCOLI AND RICE:

2⅔ cups (635 ml) water or vegan chicken broth

1⅓ cups (265 g) white rice

½ teaspoon salt, or to taste

4 cups (280 g) broccoli florets

TO MAKE THE CREAMY MUSHROOM TEMPEH:

Warm the oil in a large saucepan over medium heat. Once hot, add the yellow onions, mushrooms, and tempeh to the pan. Sauté for 5 minutes, or until the onions are translucent. Add 1 cup (235 ml) of broth to the mixture and simmer for 10 minutes, uncovered, over medium-low heat. While it's simmering, start the rice and broccoli.

Break the tempeh up into crumbles. Sprinkle the flour over the tempeh mixture, stir until everything is coated evenly, and cook for 2 minutes. Next, add the remaining 1 cup (235 ml) of broth, nondairy milk, onion powder, pepper, and sage, stirring until combined. Cover the pan with a lid and simmer for 10 minutes, stirring occasionally. Once the mixture has thickened, season with salt to taste.

TO MAKE THE RICE AND BROCCOLI:

Place the water or broth in a pot along with the rice and salt, and bring it to a boil over medium heat. Cover with a lid, and adjust the heat to medium-low. Simmer for 20 minutes, or until the rice is soft and tender.

While the rice is cooking, steam the broccoli either in a pot with a little water and a steamer basket for 10 minutes, or in the microwave in a covered bowl for 3 minutes.

To plate, divide the rice and broccoli between 4 plates or containers, and cover each with creamy mushroom tempeh.

YIELD: 4 SERVINGS

SPINACH RICOTTA STUFFED SHELLS

• MAKE AHEAD

• OIL FREE

This recipe for stuffed shells is stunningly simple and oh-so-comforting. Here we have the classic combination of spinach and ricotta, but instead of dairy, tofu and chickpeas are used for a hearty, protein-rich filling. Serve this up with a side salad and a glass of red wine, and it may just become a staple in your family dinners.

FOR THE SPINACH RICOTTA:

1 can (15 ounces, or 445 g) chickpeas, drained and rinsed

8 ounces (230 g) extra-firm tofu

¼ cup (60 g) Simple Cashew Cream (page 186)

2 tablespoons (5 g) chopped fresh basil

1 tablespoon (2 g) fresh parsley

2 teaspoons (10 ml) lemon juice

1 clove garlic, peeled

1 teaspoon salt

¼ teaspoon black pepper

½ cup (90 g) packed frozen spinach, thawed

FOR THE ASSEMBLY:

16 jumbo pasta shells

2 cups (495 g) Chunky Tomato Sauce (page 199), divided

2 tablespoons (20 g) Sunflower Parmesan (page 193)

TO MAKE THE SPINACH RICOTTA:

Place the chickpeas, tofu, Simple Cashew Cream, basil, parsley, lemon juice, garlic, salt, and pepper in a food processor equipped with an S-blade. Pulse the mixture until mostly smooth, taste, and adjust the seasonings to your preference. Squeeze excess moisture from the spinach, and fold it into the ricotta mixture. Set aside.

TO ASSEMBLE:

Preheat the oven to 350°F (180°C, or gas mark 4), and have ready a 6 x 10-inch (15 x 25 cm) or similarly sized baking dish.

Cook the jumbo shells according to the package instructions, drain, and rinse with cool water. Spread ½ cup (125 g) of Chunky Tomato Sauce over the bottom of the baking dish. Stuff each shell with spinach ricotta filling, and place it in the dish.

Once all the shells are stuffed, top them with the remaining Chunky Tomato Sauce and the Sunflower Parmesan. Bake the stuffed shells for 25 to 30 minutes, or until the sauce has bubbled and thickened slightly. Serve warm.

YIELD: 4 SERVINGS

TIP: IF YOU HAVE A LARGE GATHERING ON THE BOOKS, DOUBLE THIS RECIPE TO FIT A LARGER BAKING DISH, OR QUADRUPLE TO FIT TWO OF THEM! FOR THE LARGER SIZE, BAKE FOR 35 TO 40 MINUTES.

LEBANESE-STYLE CAULIFLOWER WITH COUSCOUS

• MAKE AHEAD

• SOY FREE • NUT FREE • SUGAR FREE

I have a couple favorite Mediterranean spots that I frequent regularly, and the cauliflower dish is a must-order. While they may fry theirs to get it extra crispy, I've baked mine to lighten it up. Pair it with an addictive tahini sauce, pita bread, and a refreshing couscous salad, and you'll be loving this dish, too.

FOR THE CAULIFLOWER:

2 pounds (910 g) cauliflower florets

2 tablespoons (30 ml) olive oil

1½ teaspoons ground cumin

½ teaspoon salt

FOR THE COUSCOUS:

1⅔ cups (395 ml) vegetable broth

1¼ cups (200 g) uncooked Israeli couscous

1 cup (190 g) diced tomatoes

½ cup (40 g) diced scallions

Pinch of salt, or to taste

FOR THE TAHINI SAUCE:

⅓ cup (80 g) tahini

¼ cup (60 ml) water

2 tablespoons (30 ml) lemon juice

½ teaspoon paprika

¼ teaspoon garlic powder

¼ teaspoon salt

3 pitas, cut into quarters

NOTE: FOR A GLUTEN-FREE ALTERNATIVE, USE 3 CUPS COOKED QUINOA IN PLACE OF THE COOKED COUSCOUS, AND SUBSTITUTE THE PITA WITH YOUR FAVORITE GLUTEN-FREE TORTILLAS.

TO MAKE THE CAULIFLOWER:

Preheat the oven to 425°F (220°C, or gas mark 7), and line a large baking sheet with parchment paper.

Place the cauliflower in a large mixing bowl, then drizzle with the olive oil. Toss to coat. Sprinkle the cauliflower with the cumin and salt, mixing again until evenly coated, then spread the florets out on a baking sheet in an even layer. Roast the cauliflower for 20 minutes, flip the florets, then roast for an additional 20 minutes, or until the cauliflower has browned edges.

TO MAKE THE COUSCOUS:

Place the broth and couscous in a pot, cover with a lid, and bring to a boil over medium heat. Adjust the heat to medium-low and simmer for 10 minutes, until the broth is absorbed and the couscous is cooked al dente.

Transfer the couscous to a bowl and chill in the refrigerator for 15 minutes. Add the tomatoes, scallions, and salt to taste, folding together until combined. Set aside.

TO MAKE THE TAHINI SAUCE:

In a small bowl, whisk the tahini, water, lemon juice, paprika, garlic powder, and salt together until very smooth.

TO ASSEMBLE:

Divide the cauliflower and couscous between 4 bowls or containers, and place 3 pita pieces in each one. Serve the sauce on the side, or drizzle it over the top of each dish.

YIELD: 4 SERVINGS

WHITE BEAN MARINARA PENNE

• UNDER 10 INGREDIENTS • 30 MINUTES OR LESS • ONE PAN
• GLUTEN-FREE OPTION • SOY FREE • NUT FREE • OIL FREE

I'm not sure it gets much easier than this penne marinara recipe! Pasta is one of my go-tos—if you haven't noticed—when it comes to making a quick dinner. Adding a savory tomato sauce, and throwing in some beans, greens, and basil, turn this into a well-rounded meal that's done in minutes.

8 ounces (225 g) penne pasta, gluten-free if necessary

2 cans (30 ounces, or 850 g) white beans, drained and rinsed

2 cups (520 g) Chunky Tomato Sauce (page 199)

1 cup (40 g) packed chopped arugula

¼ cup (10 g) chopped fresh basil, divided

Pinch of salt, or to taste

Pinch of black pepper, or to taste

Cook the penne pasta according to the package instructions. Once tender, drain and rinse the pasta, placing it back into the pot in which it was cooked. Add the white beans, Chunky Tomato Sauce, arugula, and 2 tablespoons (5 g) of basil to the pasta, bringing it to a low simmer over medium-low heat. Cook for 4 minutes, stirring occasionally.

Season the pasta with salt and pepper, if necessary. Divide it between 4 bowls, topping each with the remaining basil.

YIELD: 4 SERVINGS

TIP: IF YOU ARE GOING TO USE GLUTEN-FREE PASTA, MY FAVORITE IS BROWN RICE PASTA, BECAUSE THE TEXTURE IS QUITE LIKE SEMOLINA PASTA. MY SECOND CHOICE WOULD BE QUINOA-CORN PASTA.

TAHINI-MISO CHICKPEAS WITH ZUCCHINI

• UNDER 10 INGREDIENTS • 30 MINUTES OR LESS • MAKE AHEAD • PORTABLE
• GLUTEN FREE • NUT FREE • SUGAR FREE

When you combine tahini and miso in the same recipe, you get an umami bomb of flavor! In this dish, chickpeas are roasted with a tahini-miso coating, then enjoyed with roasted zucchini and nutty red quinoa. Sharing a sheet pan for roasting helps you with time, prep, and dishwashing!

FOR THE TAHINI-MISO CHICKPEAS:

¼ cup (50 g) tahini

1 tablespoon (15 g) mild miso paste

1 tablespoon (15 ml) tamari

2 teaspoons (10 ml) lemon juice

¼ teaspoon salt

⅛ teaspoon black pepper

2 cans (30 ounces, or 850 g) chickpeas, drained and rinsed

FOR THE ZUCCHINI:

1½ pounds (680 g) zucchini, cut into 4-inch (10 cm) spears

1 tablespoon (15 ml) olive oil

¼ teaspoon salt

¼ teaspoon black pepper

FOR THE QUINOA:

2⅔ cups (635 ml) low-sodium vegetable broth

1⅓ cups (250 g) red quinoa

TO MAKE THE TAHINI-MISO CHICKPEAS:

Preheat the oven to 375°F (190°C, or gas mark 5), and line a large baking sheet with parchment paper.

In a mixing bowl, whisk together the tahini, miso paste, tamari, lemon juice, salt, and pepper until smooth. Add the chickpeas to the bowl and fold until the chickpeas are evenly coated by the tahini mixture. Spread the chickpeas out in a single layer on one half of the baking sheet.

TO MAKE THE ZUCCHINI:

Spread the zucchini spears out in a single layer over the other half of the baking sheet, and drizzle with olive oil. Toss the spears lightly to get them coated, then sprinkle salt and pepper over them. Roast the chickpeas and zucchini for 30 minutes, stirring and flipping them halfway through.

TO MAKE THE QUINOA:

While the chickpeas and zucchini are roasting, place the vegetable broth and quinoa in a medium-sized pan, cover, and bring to a simmer over medium heat. Adjust the heat to medium-low and simmer for 18 to 20 minutes, then fluff with a spoon or fork.

To plate, divide the quinoa, zucchini, and chickpeas between 4 bowls or containers. Serve warm or refrigerate for up to 7 days.

YIELD: 4 SERVINGS

NOTE: THIS BOWL IS GREAT AS A BASE FOR YOUR FAVORITE TYPE OF SAUCE OR DRESSING. I LOVE DRIZZLING IT WITH THE TAHINI SAUCE FROM PAGE 140!

KLUSKI, A.K.A. LAZY DUMPLINGS

• UNDER 10 INGREDIENTS • 30 MINUTES OR LESS
• SOY-FREE OPTION • NUT FREE • OIL-FREE OPTION • SUGAR FREE

Right now, you may be asking yourself, "What the heck is a kluski?" A kluski is a rustic dumpling—or noodle—that is typically eaten in Eastern Europe. My dad's side of the family is Polish, so whenever we got together for a group dinner, my grandmother would make a huge batch of kluski in meat sauce for us. And though it's not sexy, she typically served it with peas and tomatoes, as seen here. Before she passed, she taught me how to make the recipe, so this veganized version is very near and dear to me. I hope that you make this on a cold winter night and are comforted by its richness.

FOR THE KLUSKI:

1 cup (235 ml) warm water

2 tablespoons (15 g) tapioca flour

2 cups (260 g) unbleached all-purpose flour

1 teaspoon nutritional yeast

¼ teaspoon salt

FOR THE ASSEMBLY:

1 tablespoon (10 g) soy-free vegan butter or coconut oil

1 cup (140 g) diced yellow onion

2 cups (310 g) cooked green or brown lentils

1½ cubes (15 g) vegan beef bouillon, crumbled

1 tablespoon (10 g) unbleached all-purpose flour

1 to 1½ cups (235-335 ml) reserved kluski-boiling water

Pinch of salt, or to taste

Pinch of black pepper, or to taste

2 cups (300 g) cooked green peas

2 large tomatoes, sliced

TO MAKE THE KLUSKI:

In a small bowl, whisk together the warm water and tapioca flour. Set aside. In a large bowl, sift the flour, nutritional yeast, and salt together until combined. Pour the tapioca mixture into the flour mixture and fold together for 1 minute.

Bring a large pot filled with roughly 2 quarts (1895 ml) of water to a boil over medium-high heat. Once at a rolling boil, spoon thumb-sized oblong dumplings into the water. I typically do this by pulling the dough up the side of the mixing bowl with a metal spoon and cutting it with the side of said spoon.

Do not overcrowd the pot, as they will expand. Boil the kluski for 3 to 4 minutes, or until they start floating on the top of the water and are opaque. Once you have cooked all the dough, place the kluski on a plate, and set aside. Do not toss out the boiling water; reserve 2 cups of it for the sauce.

TO ASSEMBLE:

In a large saucepan, warm the vegan butter over medium heat. Once hot, add the yellow onions and sauté for 5 minutes, or until the onions are translucent. Next, add the lentils to the pan, sprinkle the vegan beef bouillon and flour over the top, stir to coat everything, then cook for 2 minutes.

Add 1 cup (235 ml) of the reserved boiling water to the pan to start, and simmer over medium-low heat for 5 minutes, stirring occasionally. Once the sauce has thickened, decide if you want to add another ½ to 1 cup (120 to 235 ml) of water to thin it out more. Add the kluski to the pan and simmer, covered, for 10 minutes. Season with salt and pepper to taste.

Divide the peas and tomato slices between 4 bowls or plates, then top with the kluski-lentil mixture. Serve hot.

YIELD: 4 SERVINGS

TIP: FOR A MORE "TRADITIONAL" VERSION OF THIS RECIPE, IF AVAILABLE TO YOU, USE 2 CUPS (ROUGHLY 220 G) VEGAN BEEF CRUMBLES INSTEAD OF THE LENTILS. I DID THIS THE FIRST TIME I MADE IT VEGAN, FOR MY PARENTS, AND THEY COULDN'T BELIEVE HOW GOOD IT WAS!

LENTIL BALLS WITH ZESTY RICE

• MAKE AHEAD

• GLUTEN FREE • SOY FREE • OIL FREE • SUGAR FREE

Sometimes bean balls are served with a sauce, but I love this lighter version with zesty rice and salad. The lemon brightens the dish from what is usually a rich recipe. Going light makes this dish versatile, and something that can be enjoyed in warmer months!

FOR THE LENTIL BALLS:

2 cans (30 ounces, or 850 g) black or brown lentils, drained and rinsed

1 cup (100 g) walnut halves

3 tablespoons (5 g) chopped dried mushrooms

1½ tablespoons (25 g) tomato paste

3 tablespoons (5 g) fresh parsley

¾ teaspoon salt

½ teaspoon black pepper

½ cup (80 g) gluten-free bread crumbs

FOR THE ZESTY RICE:

2⅔ cups (635 ml) water

1⅓ cups (255 g) basmati rice

2 tablespoons (30 ml) lemon juice

1½ tablespoons (5 g) minced fresh parsley

2 teaspoons (4 g) lemon zest

⅛ teaspoon salt, or to taste

FOR THE ASSEMBLY:

2 cups (100 g) chopped lettuce

1 cup (130 g) halved cherry tomatoes

¼ cup (35 g) slivered red onion

4 lemon wedges

TO MAKE THE LENTIL BALLS:

Preheat the oven to 375°F (190°C, or gas mark 5), and line a baking sheet with parchment paper or a silicone baking mat.

Place the lentils, walnuts, dried mushrooms, tomato paste, parsley, salt, and pepper in a food processor equipped with an S-blade. Pulse the mixture until it is broken down into smaller pieces, but is not yet a paste. Fold the bread crumbs into the lentil mixture until combined.

Form twenty 2-tablespoon-sized (30 g) lentil balls with your hands, and place them on the baking sheet. Bake for 10 minutes, then flip them over and bake for an additional 10 minutes. Cool on a rack for 7 to 10 minutes before removing them.

TO MAKE THE ZESTY RICE:

In a pot, bring the water and rice to a boil over medium heat. Cover with a lid, and adjust the heat to medium-low. Simmer for 20 minutes, or until the rice is tender. Stir the lemon juice, parsley, lemon zest, and salt into the rice until evenly combined. Taste and add more salt, if preferred.

TO ASSEMBLE:

Combine the lettuce, tomatoes, and red onions in a bowl, then divide it between 4 plates or containers. Then, divide the rice and lentil balls between each plate. Garnish with a lemon wedge and serve.

YIELD: 4 SERVINGS

TIP: THE LENTIL BALLS CAN BE MADE IN BULK IN ADVANCE, THEN FROZEN FOR LATER USE!

GREEN ENCHILADA CASSEROLE

- MAKE AHEAD
- GLUTEN FREE • SOY FREE • NUT-FREE OPTION • SUGAR FREE

One year, for my birthday, I decided to make enchiladas for everyone who came over. In typical Jackie-style, I was running late after retrieving groceries, getting the house cleaned up, and decorating. Instead of taking the time to dip and roll up each enchilada, I made this casserole, and it was a hit!

FOR THE FILLING:

1 tablespoon (10 g) coconut oil

4 cups (720 g) ½-inch (1.25 cm) cubed russet potatoes

2 cups (260 g) half-moon-sliced yellow onion

2 cans (30 ounces, or 850 g) black beans, drained and rinsed

2 teaspoons (5 g) chili powder

1½ teaspoons ground cumin

1 teaspoon dried oregano

1 teaspoon salt

½ teaspoon paprika

FOR THE GREEN SAUCE:

1½ pounds (685 g) green tomatillos, chopped with husks removed

1 cup (200 g) mashed avocado

½ cup (120 ml) vegetable broth

1 jalapeño pepper, chopped with stem removed

1 serrano pepper, chopped with stem and seeds removed

3 cloves garlic, peeled

2 tablespoons (30 ml) lime juice

½ teaspoon ground cumin

1 teaspoon salt

FOR THE ASSEMBLY:

12 corn tortillas

¼ cup (60 g) Simple Cashew Cream or vegan sour cream

2 tablespoons (5 g) minced fresh cilantro

TO MAKE THE FILLING:

In a large skillet, warm the coconut oil over medium-high heat. Once hot, add the potatoes and yellow onions to the skillet and cook for 10 to 15 minutes, stirring occasionally so that multiple sides are browned. Reduce the heat to medium-low. Add the black beans, chili powder, cumin, oregano, salt, and paprika to the pan. Stir until everything is coated, and take the pan off the heat.

TO MAKE THE GREEN SAUCE:

Place all the ingredients in a blender and purée until completely smooth.

TO ASSEMBLE:

Preheat the oven to 350°F (180°C, or gas mark 4), and get out a large casserole dish.

Spoon 1 cup (235 ml) of green sauce into the bottom of the dish, and spread it out in a thin layer. Place 4 tortillas over the sauce, then top with half of the filling. Place 4 tortillas on the filling, then spoon 2 cups (475 ml) of green sauce over them, followed by the remainder of the filling, 4 more tortillas, and the last of the green sauce.

Next, drizzle Simple Cashew Cream over the top, and bake the casserole for 25 minutes, or until the edges of the tortillas start to brown and the potatoes are cooked through. Once baked, remove from the oven, garnish with cilantro, and serve.

YIELD: 8 SERVINGS

CHEEZY POTATO ONION PIEROGI

- UNDER 10 INGREDIENTS • MAKE AHEAD
- SOY-FREE OPTION • NUT-FREE OPTION • SUGAR FREE

Growing up, my father made pierogi for us many a Sunday morning. If you're not familiar with pierogi, they are stuffed dumplings that are boiled, and usually pan fried, and can be filled with potatoes, mushrooms, sauerkraut, and more. And though I do not judge my dad for reheating the frozen packaged stuff we found in the store, this version with potatoes and caramelized onions is much better!

FOR THE FILLING:

1½ cups (250 g) diced and peeled Yukon gold potatoes

1 tablespoon (15 g) soy-free vegan butter or coconut oil

1 cup (140 g) diced yellow onion

½ cup (60 g) vegan Cheddar shreds

¼ cup (60 ml) unsweetened nondairy milk

1 teaspoon garlic salt, or more to taste

¼ teaspoon black pepper, or more to taste

FOR THE DOUGH:

2 cups (260 g) unbleached all-purpose flour

¼ teaspoon salt

⅔ cup (160 ml) water

2 tablespoons (30 ml) olive oil

FOR SERVING:

2 tablespoons (30 g) soy-free vegan butter or coconut oil

½ cup (120 g) Simple Cashew Cream (page 186) or vegan sour cream, nut free if necessary

¼ cup (15 g) diced scallions

NOTE: AROUND THE HOLIDAYS, I LIKE TO MAKE A DOUBLE OR TRIPLE BATCH OF PIEROGI TO FREEZE FOR SUNDAY BRUNCH, OR EVEN DINNER!

TO MAKE THE FILLING:

Place the potatoes in a small pot and add water until they are barely covered. Bring to a boil over medium heat and cook for 8 to 10 minutes, or until the potatoes are fork tender. Drain the water from the potatoes and set the pot aside.

In a small sauté pan, warm the vegan butter over medium heat. Once hot, add the yellow onions and sauté for 15 minutes, or until mostly caramelized. Next, add the onions to the potatoes, along with the Cheddar shreds, nondairy milk, garlic salt, and pepper. Mash the potato mixture until fluffy, taste, and season with more garlic salt and pepper if need be.

TO MAKE THE DOUGH:

In a mixing bowl, sift the flour and salt together. Make a well in the middle of the dry ingredients, then add the water and oil to them. Knead the dough for 1 to 2 minutes, or until combined, with no dry spots. If the dough is still quite sticky, add a pinch or two of flour at a time and knead some more.

TO ASSEMBLE:

Lightly dust your work surface with flour, and cut the dough into 12 equal pieces—a scale comes in handy here. Roll each piece into a 4-inch (10 cm) circle, roughly 1/8 inch (3 mm) thick. Drop 2-tablespoon-sized (roughly 30 g) scoops of filling into the middle of each circle. Lightly wet the outer 1/4 inch (6 mm) of the dough rounds with water, then fold them in half. Seal the edges together by pinching them with your fingers or pressing down with a fork.

Bring a large pot filled with roughly 2 quarts (1895 ml) of water to a boil over medium-high heat. Once at a rolling boil, place 6 pierogi in the water. Do not overcrowd the pot, as they will expand slightly. Boil the pierogi for 3 to 4 minutes, or until they start floating on the top of the water and are opaque. Place the cooked pierogi on a plate, and boil the second half of the batch.

TO SERVE:

At this point, you can either freeze the pierogi for later, eat them soft, or fry them to serve. To freeze them, wait until they have cooled, then place them in a freezer-safe bag or container, laying a sheet of waxed paper down between layers. They will keep up to 6 months in the freezer.

To fry the pierogi, in a large skillet, warm the vegan butter over medium heat. Once hot, add 6 pierogi to the skillet and brown for 3 minutes on each side; repeat with the remaining 6 pierogi. Divide the pierogi between 4 plates, drizzle with Simple Cashew Cream—or serve on the side—and garnish with scallions.

YIELD: 4 SERVINGS (12 PIEROGI)

SLOW COOKER SEITAN ROAST

• UNDER 10 INGREDIENTS • MAKE AHEAD • ONE PAN
• NUT FREE • OIL FREE • SUGAR FREE

Sometimes, you just need a recipe that you can set and forget. My mother used to make slow cooker dishes all the time when I was younger—a lot of which were roasts of some kind. So, I took a note from her playbook, and made my delicious seitan round into a beautiful, hearty, slow cooker roast.

1 uncooked seitan round, from Seitan Two Ways (page 190)

2 cups (475 ml) water

2 cups (475 ml) vegan beef broth or vegetable broth

2 tablespoons (30 ml) tamari

1 cup (80 g) shiitake mushrooms

1 cup (150 g) large chop carrots, peeled

1 cup (140 g) large chop yellow onion

1 cup (170 g) fingerling potatoes

4 sprigs fresh thyme

2 sprigs fresh rosemary

Wrap the seitan round in cheesecloth, tying both ends with cooking twine. Set the seitan in the middle of a 4-quart (3.8 L) slow cooker, then pour the water, broth, and tamari around it. Place the vegetables all around the seitan, and tuck the herbs into them.

Turn the slow cooker on low, cover, and cook for 4 to 6 hours, or until the seitan is firm and the vegetables are cooked through. Once cooked, unwrap the seitan and slice it to serve. Divide the slices and vegetables between 4 plates.

YIELD: 4 SERVINGS

TIP: IF YOU LIKE YOUR SEITAN BROWNED, ONCE IT IS DONE SLOW COOKING, PLACE THE ROAST AND VEGETABLES IN AN OVEN-SAFE DISH. ROAST IT AT 375°F (190°C, OR GAS MARK 5) FOR 15 MINUTES BEFORE SERVING.

NOTE: THIS RECIPE IS GREAT FOR BULK COOKING, BECAUSE YOU CAN DOUBLE IT AND USE A LARGER SLOW COOKER FOR THE SAME RESULTS. WHEN HOLIDAYS COME AROUND, THIS IS EXTRA-USEFUL!

CHAPTER 7

FOOD ON THE MOVE

SOME ASSEMBLY REQUIRED!

Cookouts, barbecues, family parties, and the like can all be pretty dread-inducing when you first go vegan. I am here to tell you that it doesn't have to be that way. Follow these recipes when you're in a bind, and on the run!

SHAKE & BAKE BACON BRUSSELS

• UNDER 10 INGREDIENTS • PORTABLE • MAKE AHEAD
• GLUTEN FREE • SOY FREE • NUT FREE

Growing up, Shake 'n Bake was a thing, and if you're not familiar with it that may make you luckier than I. It is exactly what it sounds like: shake things in a bag and bake them, though the ingredients were questionable. Here you can make your own version, but with Brussels and bacon—two of my favorite "b" foods.

1 pound (455 g) quartered Brussels sprouts, outer leaves removed

2 tablespoons (15 ml) sunflower oil

1 tablespoon (15 ml) maple syrup

2 tablespoons (20 g) brown rice flour

1 teaspoon onion powder

½ teaspoon salt

¼ teaspoon black pepper

⅛ teaspoon cayenne pepper

½ cup (35 g) Coconut Bacon (page 195)

Preheat the oven to 400°F (200°C, or gas mark 6), and have ready a baking sheet.

In a large zip bag, place the Brussels sprouts, oil, and maple syrup. Shake the Brussels until evenly coated. In a small bowl, whisk together the brown rice flour, onion powder, salt, black pepper, and cayenne pepper. Sprinkle the dry mixture over the Brussels and shake again.

Spread the Brussels mixture over the baking sheet, and cover it with aluminum foil. Roast the Brussels for 15 minutes, remove the foil, fold in the Coconut Bacon, and roast for an additional 15 minutes, or until the leaves are browning. Serve warm!

YIELD: 4 SERVINGS

ON-THE-MOVE TIP: KEEP THE BRUSSELS SPROUTS IN A BAG WITH THE OIL AND MAPLE SYRUP. STORE THE DRY MIX AND COCONUT BACON IN A SMALL JAR. ONCE YOU'RE READY TO ROAST 'EM, ADD THE DRY MIX IN WITH THE BRUSSELS, AND PREPARE ACCORDING TO THE INSTRUCTIONS.

AT-HOME TIP: IF YOU'RE JUST MAKING THESE AT HOME, PREPARE THE BRUSSELS IN A BOWL TO CREATE LESS WASTE.

CAULIFLOWER CURRY GRILL PACKETS WITH YOGURT SAUCE

• 30 MINUTES OR LESS • PORTABLE • MAKE AHEAD
• GLUTEN FREE • SOY FREE • NUT FREE • SUGAR FREE

Every summer, I make grill packets for friends' barbecues. This way, you have a tasty and quick meal without worrying if the grill is clean. This packet is filled with curry-flavored cauliflower paired with a cool, herby yogurt sauce.

FOR THE YOGURT SAUCE:

1 cup (235 ml) plain nondairy yogurt

2 tablespoons (5 g) chopped fresh cilantro

2 tablespoons (5 g) thinly sliced scallions

1 tablespoon (15 ml) lime juice

½ teaspoon onion powder

½ teaspoon lime zest

¼ teaspoon salt

FOR THE CURRY CAULIFLOWER:

1 pound (455 g) cauliflower florets, chopped into bite-sized pieces

1 pound (455 g) russet potatoes, diced

1 cup (140 g) chopped white onion

1 cup (150 g) halved cherry tomatoes

1 cup (150 g) green peas

1 can (15 ounces, or 455 g) chickpeas, drained and rinsed

1½ tablespoons (25 ml) melted coconut oil

1½ tablespoons (10 g) curry powder

Pinch of salt, plus more to taste

Pinch of black pepper, plus more to taste

1 tablespoon (15 ml) lemon juice

TO MAKE THE YOGURT SAUCE:

Place all the yogurt sauce ingredients in a small mixing bowl, and stir until combined. Refrigerate until ready to serve.

TO MAKE THE CURRY CAULIFLOWER:

Preheat the grill to 400°F (204°C). In a very large mixing bowl, place the cauliflower, potatoes, white onions, tomatoes, peas, and chickpeas. Drizzle coconut oil over the top of the veggies, and stir until coated. Add the curry powder and a pinch of salt and pepper, and stir again until evenly coated.

Tear out 4 pieces of aluminum foil that are 12 x 18 inches (30 x 46 cm), and lay them out. Divide the curry cauliflower mixture between the 4 sheets, placing it in the middle. Fold the two long sides in toward the middle, and fold the seam together until it hits the filling. Fold the two short sides in, twice, to seal the ends.

Place each packet on the grill and cook for 7 minutes, flip them over, and grill for an additional 7 minutes. Carefully, open one packet slightly, and poke the cauliflower and potatoes to see if they are tender. If not, cook until they are. Once cooked through, place the packets on a cooling rack for 5 minutes before opening and serving. When the packets are opened, squeeze lemon juice over each one, and top with salt and pepper. Serve packets with yogurt sauce alongside and enjoy.

YIELD: 4 SERVINGS

TIP: TRY PREPARING THESE THE NIGHT BEFORE YOU GO TO A COOKOUT OR PICNIC, SO THAT THE FLAVORS REALLY GET TO MARINATE, AND YOU WON'T HAVE TO WORRY ABOUT IT THE DAY OF!

NOTE: FOR HIGHER PROTEIN CONTENT, REPLACE THE CHICKPEAS WITH 14 OUNCES (400 G) EXTRA-FIRM TOFU, DICED.

TERIYAKI ADZUKI GRILL PACKETS

• UNDER 10 INGREDIENTS • 30 MINUTES OR LESS • PORTABLE • MAKE AHEAD
• GLUTEN FREE • SOY-FREE OPTION • NUT FREE • OIL FREE

Typically, we think of teriyaki and veggies being a stir-fry, but I'm here to tell you that this grill packet is a great way to prep this flavorful pairing. I included some of my favorite veggies, but the fun part of this packet is that you can customize it however you see fit.

1 can (15 ounces, or 425 g) adzuki beans, drained and rinsed

2 cups (160 g) chopped baby bok choy

2 cups (160 g) chopped broccoli florets

3.5 ounces (100 g) shiitake mushrooms, chopped

1 cup (140 g) chopped red bell pepper

1 cup (125 g) red pearl onions

1 cup (135 g) baby corn (optional)

1 cup (235 ml) Easy Teriyaki Sauce (page 189) or store-bought, divided

Preheat the grill to 350°F (180°C), or make a campfire with an area for indirect heat, over hot coals.

In a large mixing bowl, place the beans, bok choy, broccoli, shiitake mushrooms, bell peppers, pearl onions, and baby corn (if using). Drizzle ¾ cup (175 ml) teriyaki sauce over the mixture, and toss to coat evenly. Tear out 4 pieces of aluminum foil that are 12 x 18 inches (30 x 46 cm), and lay them out.

Divide the teriyaki adzuki mixture between the 4 sheets, placing it in the middle. Fold the two long sides in toward the middle, and fold the seam together until it hits the filling. Fold the two short sides in, twice, to seal the ends.

Grill the packets for 5 minutes, then flip over and grill for 5 more minutes. Wait 2 to 3 minutes before opening, drizzling with the remaining teriyaki sauce, and serving.

YIELD: 4 SERVINGS

NOTE: FOR HIGHER PROTEIN CONTENT, REPLACE THE ADZUKI BEANS WITH 14 OUNCES (400 G) EXTRA-FIRM TOFU, DICED.

OYSTER MUSHROOM BAKE PACKETS

• UNDER 10 INGREDIENTS • 30 MINUTES OR LESS • PORTABLE • MAKE AHEAD
• GLUTEN FREE • SOY FREE • NUT FREE • SUGAR FREE

I don't know about you, but every summer I see something about someone I know going to a clam or crawfish bake. While the image of that isn't pleasant, these Oyster Mushroom Bake Packets are! They're seasoned with Old Bay and filled with summer produce to give you feelings of nostalgia.

6 ounces (170 g) oyster mushrooms, chopped

2 ears of corn, shucked and chopped into 8 pieces

2 cups (250 g) chopped zucchini

1½ cups (250 g) diced red potatoes

1 cup (140 g) chopped red onion

1 cup (150 g) chopped carrots

1 cup (120 g) chopped green beans, ends trimmed

2 tablespoons (30 ml) sunflower oil

1 tablespoon (7 g) Old Bay seasoning

1 teaspoon dulse flakes

¼ teaspoon salt

Preheat the grill to 350°F (180°C), or make a campfire with an area for indirect heat, over hot coals.

In a large mixing bowl, place the oyster mushrooms, corn pieces, zucchini, potatoes, red onions, carrots, and green beans. Drizzle the oil over the mixture, and toss to coat evenly. Sprinkle the Old Bay seasoning, dulse flakes, and salt over the top. Toss again. Tear out 4 pieces of aluminum foil that are 12 x 18 inches (30 x 46 cm), and lay them out.

Divide the oyster mushroom mixture between the 4 sheets, placing it in the middle. Fold the two long sides in toward the middle, and fold the seam together until it hits the filling. Fold the two short sides in, twice, to seal the ends.

Grill the packets for 5 minutes, then flip over and grill for 5 more minutes. Wait 2 to 3 minutes before opening and serving.

YIELD: 4 SERVINGS

NOTE: DULSE FLAKES, OR DULSE GRANULES, ARE TINY PIECES OF PURPLE SEAWEED THAT GIVE FOODS A SLIGHTLY FISHY TASTE. YOU CAN FIND THEM IN MOST ASIAN MARKETS OR SOME NATURAL FOOD STORES. IF YOU CANNOT FIND THEM, GRIND UP SOME NORI TO USE IN THEIR PLACE!

APPLE FENNEL SAUSAGE GRILL PACKETS

• UNDER 10 INGREDIENTS • 30 MINUTES OR LESS • PORTABLE • MAKE AHEAD
• NUT FREE • SUGAR FREE

Now, this grill packet was something I had put together in my mind, that I knew sounded good. But, once I made it, holy moly, it was better than I ever expected! Sliced apples, fennel, cabbage, and onion, seasoned and mixed up with savory vegan sausages, will make these packets very desirable at your next cookout.

2 cups (230 g) thinly sliced fennel

2 cups (230 g) wedged green cabbage

2 cups (235 g) thinly sliced Pink Lady apples

1½ cups (180 g) half-moon-sliced white onion

1 tablespoon (15 ml) olive oil

1 teaspoon fennel seeds

1 teaspoon salt

½ teaspoon ground sage

½ teaspoon black pepper

4 Seitan Sausages from Seitan Two Ways (page 190) or store-bought

Preheat the grill to 350°F (180°C), or make a campfire with an area for indirect heat, over hot coals.

In a large mixing bowl, place the fennel, cabbage, pink apples, and white onions. Drizzle the oil over the mixture, and toss to coat evenly. Sprinkle the fennel seeds, salt, sage, and pepper over the top. Toss again. Then, slice each sausage into ½-inch-thick (1.25 cm) rounds. Add it to the bowl and toss to combine.

Tear out 4 pieces of aluminum foil that are 12 x 18 inches (30 x 46 cm), and lay them out. Divide the sausage-veggie mixture between the 4 sheets, placing it in the middle. Fold the two long sides in toward the middle, and fold the seam together until it hits the filling. Fold the two short sides in, twice, to seal the ends.

Grill the packets for 5 minutes, then flip over and grill for 5 more minutes. Wait 2 to 3 minutes before opening and serving.

YIELD: 4 SERVINGS

CHOCOLATE CHUNK OATS ON THE GO

• UNDER 10 INGREDIENTS • 30 MINUTES OR LESS • PORTABLE • MAKE AHEAD
• GLUTEN FREE • SOY-FREE OPTION • OIL FREE

I love making this on-the-go oatmeal when I'm prepping for a weekend trip, where I'm not sure what options I'll have. This is especially helpful for family trips, where I'm the only vegan! For traveling oats, this recipe is full of flavor and rich from the dark chocolate chunks.

2 cups (220 g) gluten-free quick-cooking oats

6 tablespoons (60 g) coconut sugar

2 tablespoons (15 g) ground flaxseed

1 teaspoon ground cinnamon

¼ teaspoon salt

½ cup (70 g) dried cranberries

½ cup (75 g) chopped almonds

½ cup (40 g) chopped vegan dark chocolate, soy-free if necessary

4 cups (950 ml) boiling water, for serving

In a mixing bowl, combine the oats, coconut sugar, flaxseed, cinnamon, and salt. Divide the mixture evenly between four 16-ounce (475-ml) jars. Divide the cranberries, almonds, and dark chocolate among the jars, and seal them until ready to serve.

Once you are ready to serve, pour 1 cup boiling water into one jar, stir the mixture, place the cap on, and let the water soak in for 10 to 15 minutes. Stir again before enjoying. Repeat the process for the remaining servings as you need them. The dry mix will last up to 2 weeks in a tightly sealed jar, stored in a cool place.

YIELD: 4 SERVINGS

TIP: FOR AN EVEN MORE FILLING BREAKFAST, YOU CAN BRING A SMALL BANANA WITH YOUR DRY OATS, AND SLICE IT OVER THE TOP BEFORE ENJOYING. THIS WOULD ALSO WORK GREAT WITH A SMALL APPLE.

ASPARAGUS OMELET IN A BAG

• UNDER 10 INGREDIENTS • 30 MINUTES OR LESS • PORTABLE • MAKE AHEAD
• GLUTEN FREE • SOY FREE • NUT FREE • SUGAR FREE

An omelet may not seem like an inherently vegan dish, but this asparagus spinach omelet with a chickpea base is quite outstanding! Make this omelet-in-a-bag recipe for your next camping trip or overnight stay, so that you don't have to sacrifice quality for convenience.

1 cup (120 g) chickpea flour

3 tablespoons (15 g) nutritional yeast

2 tablespoons (15 g) cornstarch

1½ teaspoons Indian black salt (kala namak; see note on page 21)

¼ teaspoon black pepper

1¾ cups (415 ml) vegetable broth

2 cups (250 g) chopped asparagus, woody ends trimmed

1 cup (40 g) packed baby spinach or arugula

½ cup (55 g) vegan Cheddar shreds (optional)

¼ cup (30 g) diced shallots

Cooking oil spray

In a mixing bowl, whisk together the chickpea flour, nutritional yeast, cornstarch, Indian black salt, and black pepper until combined. Pour the vegetable broth into the flour mixture and whisk until smooth, then divide the mixture between 4 sealable sandwich bags.

Next, place ½ cup (75 g) of asparagus, ¼ cup (10 g) of spinach, 2 tablespoons (15 g) of Cheddar shreds (if using), and 1 tablespoon (7 g) of shallots in each bag. Store in the refrigerator or an iced cooler for up to 1 week, or move on to preparing it.

When you are ready to prepare an omelet, warm a pan or well-seasoned cast-iron skillet over medium heat. Spray the pan with a thin layer of cooking oil. Once it is hot, shake the omelet bag vigorously. Pour the mixture into the pan and cook on one side for 5 to 7 minutes, or until the edges start to brown. Flip one half over onto the other half and cook for another 2 minutes. Repeat with the remaining bags, when ready, and serve hot.

YIELD: 4 SERVINGS

TIP: IF YOU HAVE THE SPACE AND AREN'T WORRIED ABOUT WEIGHT, YOU CAN BOTTLE THESE OMELETS UP IN 12-OUNCE (355 ML) JARS.

GRILLED FRUIT SKEWERS

• UNDER 10 INGREDIENTS • 30 MINUTES OR LESS • PORTABLE • MAKE AHEAD • ONE PAN
• GLUTEN FREE • SOY FREE • NUT FREE • OIL FREE • SUGAR FREE

At parties, there's always that one mixed fruit bowl sitting there, looking delicious—but also getting skipped over. Here's a fun and easy way to present your fruit and have people grabbing it up in no time!

2 cups (300 g) large chopped pineapple

2 cups (260 g) bite-sized strawberries

2 cups (300 g) large chopped watermelon

2 cups (300 g) large chopped honeydew melon

1 cup (175 g) red grapes

1 cup (145 g) blackberries

¼ teaspoon coarse salt

Preheat the grill to 400°F (200°C) and soak 12 long wood skewers in water for 5 minutes.

In no particular order, stack the fruit on the skewers until both fruit and skewers are used up. Grill for 2 minutes on 2 sides, just until grill marks are visible. Once grilled, sprinkle salt over the top and serve.

YIELD: 6 SIDES

NOTE: THESE SKEWERS CAN BE SERVED RIGHT OFF THE GRILL, OR REFRIGERATE THEM AFTER GRILLING FOR A COOL-SMOKY EXPERIENCE.

CAMPFIRE BANANA SPLITS

• UNDER 10 INGREDIENTS   • 30 MINUTES OR LESS   • PORTABLE   • MAKE AHEAD
• GLUTEN FREE   • NUT FREE   • OIL FREE

These aren't your average banana splits! Think warm, melty, sweet, and maybe even a little gooey—if that adjective doesn't put you off too much. These sweet treats are kid-friendly and great for cooking in a little campfire.

4 bananas

¾ cup (70 g) vegan mini-marshmallows

⅓ cup (55 g) vegan chocolate chips

1 cup (120 g) sweet cherries, pitted and halved

1 teaspoon vegan sprinkles (optional)

Preheat the grill to 375°F (190°C), or make a campfire with an area for indirect heat, over hot coals.

Keeping the banana peels on, slice halfway through each banana, lengthwise. Next, stuff each banana with vegan marshmallows, chocolate chips, and sweet cherries. Wrap each banana in foil and cook for 8 to 10 minutes, allowing them to cool for 2 minutes before unwrapping them. Garnish with sprinkles, if using, and serve.

YIELD: 4 BANANA SPLITS

NOTE: IF YOU DON'T LIKE CHER-RIES, YOU CAN MAKE THIS RECIPE WITH RASPBERRIES OR CHOPPED STRAWBERRIES INSTEAD!

HERBED CORN ON THE COB

• UNDER 10 INGREDIENTS • 30 MINUTES OR LESS • PORTABLE • MAKE AHEAD
• GLUTEN FREE • SOY-FREE OPTION • NUT FREE • OIL-FREE OPTION • SUGAR FREE

For me, there's not much better than eating grilled corn in the outdoors. With this recipe, you can pack up your corn, bag up your herbs and spices, plus a little vegan butter, and hit the road. This herbed corn recipe is easy to double or triple to feed many!

4 large ears corn, shucked

2 tablespoons (30 g) soy-free vegan butter or refined coconut oil

2 tablespoons (5 g) minced fresh basil

2 tablespoons (5 g) minced fresh parsley

2 tablespoons (5 g) minced fresh cilantro

1 tablespoon (5 g) minced fresh chives

½ teaspoon salt

¼ teaspoon black pepper

Preheat the grill to 350°F (180°C), or make a campfire with an area for indirect heat, over hot coals.

Partially wrap each ear of corn in foil, leaving the top visible. Place ½ tablespoon of vegan butter on each ear; then divide the basil, parsley, cilantro, chives, salt, and pepper between them. Close the foil around the corn, then grill for 2 minutes on 4 sides.

Cool the corn packets on a rack for 5 minutes before serving.

YIELD: 4 SERVINGS

PASTRY-WRAPPED CARROT DOGS

• UNDER 10 INGREDIENTS • 30 MINUTES OR LESS • PORTABLE • MAKE AHEAD
• NUT FREE

This hotdog hack is perfect for grills, campfires, and ovens, if you prefer the indoors. You start with a simple, deliciously marinated carrot dog, wrap it up in puff pastry, and heat it over some flames. Then watch the magic happen. These are way more fun than using plain ol' hotdog buns.

8 large carrots, peeled
1 cup (235 ml) water
3 tablespoons (45 ml) tamari
2 tablespoons (30 ml) maple syrup
1 tablespoon (15 ml) apple cider vinegar
2 teaspoons (5 g) onion powder
1 teaspoon smoked paprika
1 teaspoon salt
1 sheet (245 g) vegan puff pastry
Cooking oil spray

Preheat a grill to 350°F (180°C), or make a campfire with an area for indirect heat over hot coals.

In a large saucepan, place the carrots, water, tamari, maple syrup, apple cider vinegar, onion powder, paprika, and salt. Cover with a lid and bring to a simmer over medium-low heat, simmering for 12 minutes, or until the carrots are fork tender. Pull the carrots out of the marinade, and let the excess drip off.

Cut the puff pastry into 8 even strips, lengthwise. Wrap one strip of pastry around each carrot, using a spiral motion. Place each carrot on a metal skewer and hold over indirect heat for 10 minutes, turning 45 degrees every 2 or 3 minutes, or until the puff pastry starts raising and turning golden brown.

YIELD: 8 CARROT DOGS

NOTE: YOU CAN ALSO BAKE THESE IN THE OVEN AT 350°F (180°C) FOR 12 TO 15 MINUTES, OR UNTIL THE PUFF PASTRY TURNS GOLDEN BROWN. SERVE WARM.

ON-THE-MOVE TIP: IF YOU'RE PLANNING ON TAKING THESE CARROT DOGS ON A TRIP, FOLLOW THE INSTRUCTIONS UNTIL AFTER THE CARROTS ARE SIMMERED. THEN, STORE THE CARROTS IN A CONTAINER OR ZIP BAG WITH ½ CUP (120 ML) OF MARINADE. BRING A DEFROSTED SHEET OF PUFF PASTRY WITH YOU, BUT KEEP REFRIGERATED—FOR UP TO 5 DAYS—BEFORE USE.

PEANUT BUTTER S'MORES DIP

- UNDER 10 INGREDIENTS • 30 MINUTES OR LESS • PORTABLE • MAKE AHEAD • ONE PAN
- GLUTEN FREE • SOY FREE • OIL FREE

S'mores is a quintessential camping food, and though I love it so, I thought it could use an upgrade. This dip is rich with chocolate, swirled with peanut butter, and topped with marshmallows ripe for toasting. Dunk your graham cracker in, and start the dessert party!

9 ounces (255 g) vegan chocolate chips

¾ cup (195 g) creamy peanut butter

10 ounces (28 g) large vegan marshmallows

2 tablespoons (20 g) crushed roasted peanuts

½ teaspoon coarse salt

8 ounces (220 g) gluten-free vegan graham crackers

Preheat the grill or oven to 400°F (200°C), and have ready an 8-inch (20 cm) cast-iron skillet.

Spread the chocolate chips over the bottom of the skillet, and spoon dollops of peanut butter throughout them. Cover the chocolate chips and peanut butter with the marshmallows. Grill or bake for 11 to 13 minutes, or until the marshmallow tops have browned and the chocolate is melted.

Sprinkle peanuts and salt over the top of the dip. Serve warm with graham crackers.

YIELD: 8 SERVINGS

CHEATER CHILAQUILES

• 30 MINUTES OR LESS • PORTABLE • MAKE AHEAD • ONE PAN
• GLUTEN FREE • SOY FREE • NUT FREE • OIL FREE • SUGAR FREE

There are already walking tacos and Frito pies in a bag, but these Cheater Chilaquiles can take them out in a single bite! Here I show you a shortcut to making a delicious ancho chile sauce in a fraction of the time it usually would take. Plus, you can take these with you for a picnic or beach trip.

FOR THE ANCHO CHILI SAUCE:

1 cup (235 ml) tomato sauce

1 cup (235 ml) vegetable broth

¾ cup (100 g) chopped white onion

2 tablespoons (30 g) diced serrano pepper

1 tablespoon (5 g) ancho chile powder

1 clove garlic, peeled

½ teaspoon salt, or to taste

FOR THE BEAN SALSA:

1 can (15 ounces, or 425 g) black beans, drained and rinsed

1 cup (170 g) cooked corn kernels

¼ cup (40 g) diced red onion

2 tablespoons (5 g) minced fresh cilantro

1½ tablespoons (25 ml) lime juice

¼ teaspoon salt, or to taste

FOR THE ASSEMBLY:

1 bag (8 ounces, or 225 g) corn tortilla chips

¼ cup (30 g) vegan mozzarella shreds

TO MAKE THE ANCHO CHILI SAUCE:

Place the tomato sauce, broth, white onions, serrano pepper, ancho chile powder, garlic, and salt in a blender. Purée until smooth. Transfer the mixture to a large saucepan, and simmer over medium-low heat for 10 minutes, stirring occasionally.

TO MAKE THE BEAN SALSA:

In a medium mixing bowl, combine the black beans, corn, red onions, cilantro, lime juice, and salt until mixed. Refrigerate until ready to assemble.

TO ASSEMBLE:

Pour the warm—but not too hot—ancho chili sauce into the bag of chips. Hold the opening closed, and shake the chips around until well coated. Divide the chips between 4 plates or bowls, top with bean salsa, and finish with mozzarella shreds.

YIELD: 4 SERVINGS

ON-THE-MOVE TIP: TO TAKE THIS DISH ON THE GO, BOTTLE THE SAUCE UP AFTER SIMMERING IT, AND TRAVEL WITH THAT, THE JAR OF BEAN SALSA, A BAG OF CHIPS, AND A BAG OF VEGAN CHEESE. IT'S SUPER EASY TO REASSEMBLE AND SERVE!

FOILED STRAWBERRY FRENCH TOAST

• PORTABLE • MAKE AHEAD
• SOY FREE • OIL FREE

Who ever thought campfire food could be this fancy? After trying this recipe out, I'm almost sure that I'll be making French toast this way—even when I'm at home! This brunch idea is great for feeding a group a delicious meal with little effort involved.

1 can (13.5 ounces, or 400 ml) full-fat coconut milk

¼ cup (40 g) chickpea flour

3 tablespoons (45 ml) maple syrup

1 tablespoon (5 g) nutritional yeast

2 teaspoons (10 ml) vanilla extract

1 teaspoon ground cinnamon

½ teaspoon Indian black salt (kala namak; see note on page 21)

1 pound (455 g) loaf of French bread

2 cups (290 g) sliced fresh strawberries

½ cup (30 g) chopped pecans

2 tablespoons (15 g) powdered sugar

Preheat the grill to 350°F (180°C), or make a campfire with an area for indirect heat, over hot coals.

In a blender, purée the coconut milk, chickpea flour, maple syrup, nutritional yeast, vanilla, ground cinnamon, and Indian black salt until smooth. Either pour the mixture into a zip bag or jar for later use, or set aside and prep the loaf of bread.

Cut 1-inch (3 cm) thick slices into the bread, leaving the bottom ½ inch (1.25 cm) intact. Cut a piece of foil large enough to wrap around the entire loaf, and set the loaf in the middle of it. Fold the foil up to create 4 walls up against the loaf, then pour the coconut milk mixture over the top and in between the slices of bread.

Fold the foil all the way over, crimp the seams, and fold them over until it is all sealed. Place the loaf on the grill for 10 minutes, then roll it 120 degrees and cook for another 10 minutes, then roll it to the third and final side and cook for 10 more minutes.

Take the French toast loaf off the grill, and peel the foil apart. Top with fresh strawberries and pecans, and sprinkle with powdered sugar. Serve warm.

YIELD: 8 SERVINGS

TIP: IF YOU LIKE YOUR FRENCH TOAST ON THE CRISPIER SIDE, COOK THIS LOAF FOR 12 TO 15 MINUTES ON EACH SIDE, INSTEAD OF 10.

CHIMICHURRI PORTOBELLO TACOS

• MAKE AHEAD • ONE PAN • PORTABLE
• GLUTEN FREE • SOY FREE • NUT FREE • SUGAR FREE

Mushrooms are so versatile, and this recipe is no different. Marinated in a fresh chimichurri sauce, once grilled, these portobello mushrooms become juicy and tender—perfect for making tacos with. Share the love by bagging the marinated 'shrooms and taking them with you to cook with friends for Taco Night.

FOR THE CHIMICHURRI PORTOBELLOS:

1 cup (20 g) fresh cilantro
1 cup (20 g) fresh parsley
¼ cup (5 g) fresh oregano
¼ cup (60 ml) olive oil
¼ cup (60 ml) red wine vinegar
2 cloves garlic, peeled
½ teaspoon salt, or to taste
½ teaspoon crushed red pepper
12 ounces (340 g) portobello mushrooms

FOR THE TACOS:

8 corn tortillas
½ cup (70 g) minced white onion
¼ cup (5 g) minced fresh cilantro
¼ cup (30 g) thinly sliced radishes
1 cup (180 g) cubed avocado
8 small lemon wedges

TO MAKE THE CHIMICHURRI PORTOBELLOS:

Preheat the grill to 375°F (190°C).

Place the cilantro, parsley, oregano, olive oil, red wine vinegar, garlic, salt, and red pepper in a blender or food processor equipped with an S-blade. Pulse until the mixture is mostly smooth and the herbs are broken up into small pieces.

Cut the portobello mushrooms into ½-inch (1.25 mm) slices, and place them in a large zip bag or a container with a lid. Pour the chimichurri sauce over the top of the mushrooms, then gently toss them to coat evenly. Set them aside to marinate for 30 minutes.

Grill the portobello strips for 4 to 5 minutes on both flat sides until the mushrooms are tender with visible grill marks. You may want to use a grill pan if the grates on your grill are too wide.

TO MAKE THE TACOS:

Warm the corn tortillas on the grill for 30 seconds on both sides to make them pliable. Divide the portobellos between the tortillas, and top each with onions, cilantro, radish slices, and avocado. Serve each taco with a lemon wedge.

YIELD: 8 TACOS

ON-THE-MOVE TIP: TO TAKE THESE TACOS ON THE GO, LEAVE THE MUSHROOMS IN THE MARINADE CONTAINER AND MIX YOUR TOPPINGS TOGETHER TO TAKE IN A JAR!

BEER CAN PULLED CABBAGE

- PORTABLE
- GLUTEN-FREE OPTION • SUGAR FREE

A couple of years ago, I watched a cooking video on beer can cabbage, and after a couple of tries, I figured out a version that I really love, and I think you will, too. This beer can pulled cabbage is coated in a Thai-inspired peanut butter–sriracha barbecue sauce, and served up with a chilled, garlic mayo slaw!

FOR THE BEER CAN PULLED CABBAGE:

Small head of red cabbage

1 can (12 ounces, or 355 ml) beer, 2 tablespoons (30 ml) reserved (I used an amber ale.)

1 cup (235 ml) vegan barbecue sauce

¼ cup (65 g) creamy peanut butter

3 tablespoons (45 g) sriracha or similar chili garlic sauce

2 tablespoons (30 ml) lime juice

FOR THE ASSEMBLY:

1 cup (60 g) shredded lettuce

1 cup (90 g) grated carrots

¼ cup (60 g) Garlic Mayo (page 193) or vegan mayo

Pinch of salt

6 ciabatta or hamburger buns, gluten-free, if necessary

1 tablespoon (5 g) black sesame seeds

ON-THE-MOVE TIP: TO BRING THIS AWESOME DISH TO A PARTY, PREP THE BARBECUE SAUCE MIXTURE AND SLAW BEFOREHAND; THAT WAY YOU CAN JUST BRING A HEAD OF CABBAGE, A BEER, A JAR OF SAUCE, AND YOUR TOPPINGS.

TO MAKE THE BEER CAN PULLED CABBAGE:

Preheat the grill to 400°F (200°C).

Remove the core of the cabbage and carve out enough cabbage to be able to place it halfway down on the beer can. Place the cabbage on top of the open beer can. In a small bowl, whisk together the barbecue sauce, peanut butter, sriracha, and lime juice until combined. Reserve ½ cup (120 ml) for serving.

Brush a layer of the sauce all over the cabbage and place it on a steady part of the grill, so that it does not fall over. You can also put a small, resilient baking sheet underneath the beer can if the grate is too unstable.

Lower the lid of your grill, and cook the cabbage for 1 hour, brushing it with the barbecue sauce mixture every 15 minutes. If your grill has a hot spot, make sure to rotate the cabbage every 15 minutes, so that it cooks evenly. While this is cooking, make the slaw.

Once there is some char on the outside and the cabbage is tender, carefully remove the cabbage and can from the grill. Place the cabbage on a cutting board, cut ¼-inch (6 mm) slices down through the cabbage, then transfer it to a mixing bowl. Toss the cabbage with the reserved barbecue sauce, plus the reserved beer; set aside until ready to assemble.

In a small bowl, make a slaw by combining the lettuce, carrots, Garlic Mayo, and salt.

TO ASSEMBLE:

Toast the buns, if that is your preference. Divide the pulled cabbage between the buns, topping it with slaw and black sesame seeds. Serve warm.

YIELD: 6 SANDWICHES

TEMPEH-STUFFED POBLANO PEPPERS

• UNDER 10 INGREDIENTS • PORTABLE • MAKE AHEAD
• GLUTEN FREE • OIL FREE • SUGAR FREE

Stuffed peppers can be cute and filled with all kinds of wonderful foods, so why not make them fire-friendly? Here we have tasty poblano peppers stuffed with satiating tempeh-pecan crumbles, and a few veggies. Wrap them in foil and toss them on the grill, or put them over coals, to have single-serving dinners on-the-go!

1 cup (235 ml) vegetable broth, divided
8 ounces (225 g) tempeh, chopped
½ cup (70 g) diced yellow onion
1 clove garlic, minced
½ cup (120 ml) tomato sauce
½ cup (50 g) chopped pecans
1 cup (40 g) baby spinach
½ cup (75 g) green peas
2 tablespoons (15 g) sliced green olives
¼ to ½ teaspoon salt
¼ teaspoon black pepper
4 poblano peppers, slit open lengthwise, stemmed, and hollowed

Preheat the grill to 350°F (180°C), or make a campfire with an area for indirect heat, over hot coals.

Pour ½ cup (120 ml) of vegetable broth into a sauté pan, and bring it to a simmer over medium heat. Once simmering, add the tempeh and yellow onions, sautéing for 3 to 5 minutes, or until the onions are mostly translucent. Add the remaining vegetable broth, garlic, tomato sauce, and pecans to the pan. Adjust the heat to medium-low, cover with a lid, and simmer for 5 minutes.

Next, add the spinach, green peas, and olives, cooking until the spinach has wilted. Season with salt and pepper, to taste. Once all the liquid has been absorbed, pack the tempeh mixture into the 4 peppers.

Wrap each one in foil and place on the grill, cooking for 15 minutes—5 minutes on 3 sides of the pepper—or until the pepper is tender, with some grill marks. Set the peppers aside to cool for 3 minutes before serving.

YIELD: 4 STUFFED PEPPERS

ON-THE-MOVE TIP: PREP THESE PEPPERS AHEAD OF TIME BY STUFFING THEM, THEN WRAP THEM IN FOIL. STORED IN A REFRIGERATOR, AND GRILL WITHIN 4 OR 5 DAYS.

HEARTY LENTIL RICE SOUP MIX

• PORTABLE • MAKE AHEAD
• GLUTEN FREE • SOY FREE • NUT FREE • OIL FREE • SUGAR FREE

A dry soup mix is great for taking camping or keeping in your earthquake kit in case of emergencies. This soup mix is made up of hearty lentils and mushrooms, plus beautiful black pearl rice, and some of my favorite herbs and spices.

1 cup (200 g) black pearl rice or wild rice
¾ cup (150 g) dried green lentils
½ cup (15 g) dried porcini mushrooms
½ cup (10 g) dried shiitake mushrooms
¼ cup (20 g) dried chopped onions
1 teaspoon dried garlic granules
1 teaspoon dried rosemary
1 teaspoon dried thyme
1 teaspoon salt, or more to taste
½ teaspoon black pepper, or more to taste
½ teaspoon dried marjoram
½ teaspoon ground mustard
¼ teaspoon celery seed
8 cups (1920 ml) water

Place all the ingredients, except for the water, in a 32-ounce (945 ml) jar that you can seal tightly.

Once you are ready to cook the soup, place the jar contents in a large soup pot, along with the water. Bring to a boil over medium-high heat. Cover with a lid, adjust the heat to medium, and bring it to a simmer. Cook for 40 to 45 minutes, stirring occasionally, or until the lentils and rice are cooked all the way through.

Taste the soup and season with more salt or pepper, if you see fit. Serve hot.

YIELD: 6 TO 8 SERVINGS

ON-THE-MOVE TIP: IF YOU WANT TO DOLE THESE OUT INTO INDIVIDUAL SERVINGS INSTEAD OF MAKING ONE BIG BATCH, DIVIDE THE INGREDIENTS BETWEEN 6 ZIP BAGS TO CARRY WITH YOU.

CHAPTER 8

MAKE YOUR OWN STAPLES

QUALITY OVER CONVENIENCE, IF TIME ALLOWS

I get it. Buying premade dressings and vegan products can be a total lifesaver! This chapter of basics is for when you have an extra moment to stock your fridge with homemade staples. You won't regret it, once you taste the difference.

BUCKWHEAT TACO MEAT

• 30 MINUTES OR LESS • MAKE AHEAD
• GLUTEN FREE • SOY FREE • NUT FREE • SUGAR FREE

Over the last couple of years I've fallen deeply in love with buckwheat. I know it's an unusual romance, but after seeing its versatility from sweet to savory recipes, I'm enamored. Now, I have created a spicy taco meat with this grain. It is chewy and nutty, and it works well in so many dishes.

1 tablespoon (15 ml) sunflower oil

1 cup (180 g) raw buckwheat, groats

1¼ cups (295 ml) vegetable broth

1 teaspoon ancho chile powder

1 teaspoon ground cumin

1 teaspoon onion powder

½ teaspoon garlic powder

½ teaspoon dried oregano

¼ teaspoon ground coriander

¼ teaspoon paprika

Pinch of cayenne pepper

½ teaspoon salt, or to taste

2 teaspoons (10 ml) lime juice

In a large pan or skillet, warm the oil over medium heat. Once hot, add the buckwheat groats and stir them around, coating them in oil. Toast the grains for 3 to 5 minutes, or until their edges start to darken.

Add the vegetable broth, ancho chile powder, cumin, onion powder, garlic powder, oregano, coriander, paprika, and cayenne pepper to the pan, and bring to a simmer. Then, adjust the heat to medium-low and simmer for 10 minutes, stirring occasionally, or until the buckwheat groats are cooked al dente.

Season with salt, to taste. Drizzle lime juice over the groats, stirring to incorporate it well. Use while warm, or store in a tightly sealed container for up to 1 week in the refrigerator.

YIELD: 2 CUPS (350 G)

SIMPLE CASHEW CREAM

• UNDER 10 INGREDIENTS • 30 MINUTES OR LESS • PORTABLE • MAKE AHEAD
• GLUTEN FREE • SOY FREE • OIL FREE • SUGAR FREE

You can't get more basic than this cashew cream, or else you'd just have water. This cream can make dishes instantly luscious, and it is so versatile! I love it in my Creamy Berry-Full Polenta (page 22) and Spinach Ricotta Stuffed Shells (page 138).

1 cup (140 g) raw cashews
⅓ to ½ cup (80 to 120 ml) water
Pinch of salt

Soak the cashews in boiling water for 15 minutes. Drain and rinse the cashews, then place them in a blender with ⅓ cup (80 ml) water, to start, plus salt. Blend until completely smooth, adding more water if your blender is struggling.

Refrigerate until ready to use; it will continue to thicken as it cools. It will keep for 7 to 10 days in the refrigerator.

YIELD: APPROXIMATELY 1 CUP (240 G)

TIP: IF YOU RUN OUT OF NONDAIRY MILK, MAKE SOME ON THE FLY! MIX 1 TABLESPOON (15 G) OF CASHEW CREAM WITH 8 OUNCES (235 ML) OF WATER AND SHAKE VIGOROUSLY.

BERRY RHUBARB CHIA JAM

• UNDER 10 INGREDIENTS • 30 MINUTES OR LESS • PORTABLE • MAKE AHEAD • ONE PAN
• GLUTEN FREE • SOY FREE • NUT FREE • OIL FREE

It may seem odd, but I'm more likely to have fruit in my freezer, than jam in my refrigerator. Out of this "problem" came this incredibly delectable Berry Rhubarb Chia Jam. It has a lot less sugar than your average jam or jelly. Plus, rhubarb is a vegetable—that must count for something, right?

1 cup (140 g) blueberries
1 cup (155 g) chopped strawberries
1 cup (120 g) chopped rhubarb
½ cup (115 ml) water
1 tablespoon (15 ml) maple syrup
¼ cup (40 g) chia seeds

Place the blueberries, strawberries, rhubarb, water, and maple syrup in a saucepan. Bring to a boil over medium heat. Adjust the heat to medium-low and simmer for 10 minutes, gently stirring occasionally. Stir in the chia seeds and set aside for 5 to 10 minutes, or until the chia seeds become soft.

Store in a tightly sealed jar or container in the refrigerator for up to 2 weeks.

YIELD: 2 CUPS (560 G)

EASY TERIYAKI SAUCE

• UNDER 10 INGREDIENTS • 30 MINUTES OR LESS • MAKE AHEAD • ONE PAN
• GLUTEN FREE • SOY-FREE OPTION • NUT FREE • OIL FREE

My boyfriend is a huge fan of pretty much anything teriyaki, so how could I not make a few dishes just for him? This quick teriyaki sauce comes together rapidly and with ease, using ingredients that everyone has on hand.

2 cups (475 ml) water, divided
10 tablespoons (120 g) brown sugar
½ cup (120 ml) tamari or coconut aminos
¼ cup (60 ml) agave nectar
½ teaspoon ground ginger
½ teaspoon garlic powder
2½ tablespoons (25 g) cornstarch
2 tablespoons (20 g) toasted sesame seeds

Place 1 cup (235 ml) of water, brown sugar, tamari, agave nectar, ginger, and garlic in a small saucepan. Bring to a boil over medium heat. Adjust the heat to medium-low and simmer for 3 minutes, stirring occasionally, until the sugar is dissolved.

In a small bowl, whisk together the remaining water and the cornstarch, then add it to the saucepan. Whisk until the mixture is combined, then stir in the sesame seeds. Simmer for 3 to 5 minutes, or until the cornstarch activates and thickens the teriyaki sauce.

Transfer to a tightly sealed jar or container, and refrigerate for up to 2 weeks.

YIELD: 2½ CUPS (600 ML)

SEITAN TWO WAYS

• PORTABLE • MAKE AHEAD
• NUT FREE • SUGAR FREE

I remember the first time I made seitan at home. I hadn't yet bought some from the store, only enjoyed it in restaurants, and I was so excited. Only years later did I realize that homemade seitan is roughly one thousand times better than store-bought, and it is both cheaper to make and more delicious! Here I show you two ways to make seitan that will prove to be very useful not only for this book, but in life.

FOR THE SEITAN BASE:

1½ cups (185 g) vital wheat gluten

⅓ cup (35 g) tapioca flour

3 tablespoons (15 g) nutritional yeast

1 teaspoon garlic powder

1 teaspoon sodium-free poultry seasoning

½ teaspoon smoked paprika

¼ teaspoon black pepper

1 cup (235 ml) vegetable broth

2½ tablespoons (40 ml) tamari

1 tablespoon (15 ml) olive oil

½ tablespoon tomato paste

FOR THE PRESSURE COOKER SEITAN ROUND:

3 cups (720 ml) vegetable broth

2 cups (475 ml) water

¼ cup (60 ml) tamari

1 teaspoon onion powder

TO MAKE THE SAUSAGES:

Preheat the oven to 350°F (180°C, or gas mark 4), and have ready a baking sheet.

In a mixing bowl, whisk together the vital wheat gluten, tapioca flour, nutritional yeast, garlic powder, poultry seasoning, paprika, and black pepper. In a smaller bowl, combine the vegetable broth, tamari, olive oil, and tomato paste, whisking until smooth. Add the wet mixture to the dry and knead for 3 minutes, or until the seitan is springy and slightly firm.

Divide the seitan into 4 equal pieces, rolling them into rough sausage shapes. Wrap each one in foil, creating a sausage roughly 1 inch (2.5 cm) in diameter, and twist the foil on the ends to bring it taut. Place the sausages on the baking sheet and bake for 30 to 32 minutes, or until the sausages feel firm when poked.

Allow the sausages to cool for 15 minutes on a rack before removing them from their wrappers.

TO MAKE THE PRESSURE COOKER SEITAN ROUND:

In a mixing bowl, whisk together the vital wheat gluten, tapioca flour, nutritional yeast, garlic powder, poultry seasoning, paprika, and black pepper. In a smaller bowl, combine 1 cup (235 ml) of vegetable broth, 2½ tablespoons (40 ml) of tamari, olive oil, and tomato paste, whisking until smooth. Add the wet mixture to the dry and knead for 3 minutes, or until the seitan is springy and slightly firm.

Form the seitan into a "roast" shape—oblong and roughly 3 inches (7.5 cm) in diameter. Wrap it in cheesecloth, tying the ends with cooking twine, to create a candy wrapper

effect. Place the seitan in a pressure cooker, and add 3 cups (720 ml) of vegetable broth, 2 cups (475 ml) of water, ¼ cup (60 ml) of tamari, and onion powder to the pot.

Secure the lid and bring up to high pressure over medium-high heat. Once pressure is reached, adjust the heat to medium-low and set a timer for 25 minutes. After the timer goes off, release the pressure, and remove the lid, once safe. Place the seitan round in a container and refrigerate for at least 2 hours before removing the cheesecloth and slicing, for the best texture and deli slices.

YIELD: 4 SAUSAGES OR ONE 1¼ POUND (570 G) SEITAN ROUND

NOTE: YOU CAN USE THE LEFTOVER STOCK FROM THE PRESSURE COOKER SEITAN AS A VEGAN BEEF STOCK FOR SOUPS, OR FOR AN AU JUS-STYLE DIP FOR THE STUFFED DELI SANDWICH (SEE PAGE 86).

GARLIC MAYO

• 10 INGREDIENTS OR LESS • 30 MINUTES OR LESS • MAKE AHEAD • ONE PAN
• GLUTEN FREE • NUT FREE

Making your own mayo is as easy as dumping a few ingredients in a blender and giving it a whirl! You'll be using this protein-rich mayo in tons of dishes throughout this book, like pesto aioli (page 83) or the slaw in the BBQ Tempeh Wrap (page 69).

1 package (12 ounces, or 340 g) silken tofu
¼ cup (60 ml) sunflower oil
¼ cup (60 ml) white vinegar
2 cloves garlic, peeled
¾ teaspoon salt
½ tablespoon agave nectar

Place all the ingredients in a blender, and purée until very smooth. Transfer the mayo to a tightly sealed jar or container, and refrigerate for up to 2 weeks.

YIELD: 1¾ CUPS (420 G)

NOTE: LEAVE OUT THE GARLIC FOR A VERSATILE VEGAN MAYO THAT YOU CAN CUSTOMIZE HOWEVER YOU LIKE!

SUNFLOWER PARMESAN

• UNDER 10 INGREDIENTS • 30 MINUTES OR LESS • MAKE AHEAD • ONE PAN
• GLUTEN FREE • SOY-FREE OPTION • NUT FREE • OIL FREE • SUGAR FREE

There are many recipes for vegan Parmesan in the world, but I'm a big fan of this nut-free version that includes some miso paste for a little more tang. You'll love this Sunflower Parmesan on Spinach Ricotta Stuffed Shells (page 138) and so much more!

1 cup (145 g) raw sunflower seeds
2 tablespoons (10 g) nutritional yeast, or more to taste
1½ teaspoons white miso paste or chickpea miso
¼ teaspoon salt, or more to taste

Place all the ingredients in a food processor equipped with an S-blade. Pulse until the mixture resembles small grains; taste and add more salt or nutritional yeast, if preferred. Transfer to a tightly sealed jar or container, and refrigerate for up to 2 weeks.

YIELD: 1½ CUPS (155 G)

COCONUT BACON

• UNDER 10 INGREDIENTS   • 30 MINUTES OR LESS   • MAKE AHEAD   • ONE PAN
• GLUTEN FREE   • SOY FREE   • NUT FREE   • OIL FREE

If you're ever craving smoky, sweet, salty deliciousness, look no further. This Coconut Bacon is something that I'm extremely proud of, especially because it is very allergy friendly. Try it out on the Coconut BLT+P (page 80) or on some pita pizzas (page 124)!

1 cup (60 g) unsweetened coconut flakes
4 teaspoons (20 ml) maple syrup
2 teaspoons (10 ml) liquid smoke
¾ teaspoon salt
½ teaspoon onion powder
½ teaspoon garlic powder
¼ teaspoon smoked paprika
⅛ teaspoon black pepper

Preheat the oven to 350°F (180°C, or gas mark 4), and line a small baking sheet with parchment paper.

In a mixing bowl, place the coconut flakes, maple syrup, liquid smoke, salt, onion powder, garlic powder, smoked paprika, and black pepper. Toss the mixture until everything is evenly coated, then spread it out in a single layer over the parchment paper.

Bake for 5 minutes, stir the bacon around, and bake for an additional 5 minutes, or until the coconut bacon is amber brown. If not using right away, store in a tightly sealed jar in the refrigerator for up to 3 weeks. Let it reach room temperature once you take it out to use it.

YIELD: 1 CUP (70 G)

BUTTERNUT CHEESE SAUCE

• UNDER 10 INGREDIENTS • 30 MINUTES OR LESS • MAKE AHEAD
• GLUTEN FREE • SOY FREE • NUT FREE • SUGAR FREE

If it were up to me, I'd cover almost everything in this Butternut Cheese Sauce, and after you try it, I think you'll feel similarly. I know it's hard to imagine a vegan cheese sauce without nutritional yeast or cashews, but it's here and it is mighty flavorful. Try it out on Butternut Mac and Trees (page 103) or on the Party Nacho Platter (page 114).

1 cup (140 g) peeled and chopped butternut squash

⅔ cup (120 g) chopped Yukon gold potatoes

½ cup (70 g) chopped yellow onion

1 tablespoon (15 g) chopped roasted red pepper

4 teaspoons (20 ml) olive oil

1 clove garlic, peeled

1 teaspoon apple cider vinegar

1 teaspoon salt

½ teaspoon lemon juice

Place the squash, potatoes, and onion in a small pot, then add enough water to just barely cover them. Cover the pot with a lid and bring to a boil over medium heat, then adjust the heat to medium-low and simmer for 10 to 12 minutes, or until the potatoes are fork tender.

Drain the liquid, reserving ½ cup (120 ml). Place the squash, potatoes, yellow onions, red peppers, olive oil, garlic, apple cider vinegar, salt, and lemon juice in a blender. Pour the reserved boiling liquid in, and blend until completely smooth. Use immediately, or store in a tightly sealed jar in the refrigerator for up to 1 week.

YIELD: 2 CUPS (475 ML)

NUT-FREE PEPITA PESTO

• UNDER 10 INGREDIENTS • 30 MINUTES OR LESS • MAKE AHEAD • ONE PAN
• GLUTEN FREE • SOY FREE • NUT FREE • SUGAR FREE

When it comes to sauces, pesto is a vibrant, green stunner that goes great with so many foods. This pesto is nut free, made with pepitas instead of the pine nuts you'd typically find in a pesto. Plus, we are using kale, every vegan's favorite green—insert winky face.

2 cups (75 g) chopped kale, packed

¾ cup (105 g) raw pepitas (shelled pumpkin seeds)

1 cup (30 g) packed fresh basil leaves

5 tablespoons (75 ml) olive oil

3 tablespoons (15 g) nutritional yeast

¼ cup (60 ml) water

2 tablespoons (30 ml) lemon juice

2 cloves garlic, peeled

1 tablespoon (20 g) chickpea miso

½ teaspoon salt

¼ teaspoon black pepper

Place all the ingredients in a food processor equipped with an S-blade, and pulse until mostly smooth. Taste the pesto and add more seasonings as you see fit, if necessary.

Store the pesto in a tightly sealed jar in the refrigerator for up to 1 week.

YIELD: 1½ CUPS (375 G)

NOTE: YOU CAN MAKE THIS PESTO WITH ALMOST ANY GREEN. I LOVE MAKING IT WITH ARUGULA OR SPINACH AS WELL AS THIS KALE VERSION.

CHUNKY TOMATO SAUCE

• UNDER 10 INGREDIENTS • 30 MINUTES OR LESS • MAKE AHEAD • ONE PAN
• GLUTEN FREE • SOY FREE • NUT FREE • OIL FREE

Whether it be on pizzas or over pasta, you'll find yourself making big batches of this sauce to have on hand at all times. Forget paying too much for simple jarred sauces—you can make this Chunky Tomato Sauce in a jiff, without even trying.

1 can (15 ounces, or 425 g) tomato sauce

1 can (14.5 ounces, or 410 g) diced tomatoes

1 tablespoon (15 g) tomato paste

1 clove garlic, minced

1 teaspoon sugar

½ teaspoon dried oregano

½ teaspoon dried basil

¼ teaspoon crushed red pepper (optional)

¼ teaspoon salt, or to taste

Place the tomato sauce, diced tomatoes, tomato paste, garlic, sugar, oregano, basil, and crushed red pepper (if using) in a saucepan. Bring it to a low boil over medium heat. Adjust the heat to medium-low and simmer for 10 minutes, stirring occasionally.

Taste the tomato sauce and season with salt, to preference. Use immediately, or store in a tightly sealed container for up to 1 week in the refrigerator.

YIELD: 3 CUPS (740 G)

ACKNOWLEDGMENTS

This is book number two, so I don't want to get too redundant with my thank yous, but there are still so many people I'd love to mention. These people have helped me via either supporting my goals, or helping me physically, emotionally, or mentally.

To my parents, thank you for your continued support, for believing in me, and for testing out so many of the recipes I put in front of you without much context, plus occasionally washing some dishes. I definitely could not do this without you, and I'm sure you know that!

Thank you to my sisters and extended family for listening to my rants, helping with book tours, and giving me perspective. To Corey, book number one was hard, but this one was harder. Your understanding and support help me so much more than I can express, and I love you so much!

Michelle, my assistant, kudos to you for trying to wrangle this tornado of food, messy writing, and overbooking. Thank you for all your help through this project.

To all my friends: Damn, thank you for staying with me through the months where I'm cooped up in my kitchen or at my desk, working for weeks at a time with no fun planned in between. Here's to better work-life balance in the future!

A huge thank you to my recipe testers; you play such a huge role in the cookbook writing process, in making sure these recipes are quality. I appreciate you, and you are the best!

Lastly, thank you to UKonserve for sending me the amazing reusable containers and sandwich packets pictured on pages 8, 19, 71, 81, 82, 89, 90, and 142! They are so perfect for putting meals together on the go, and your contribution is appreciated.

ABOUT THE AUTHOR

Jackie Sobon is the creator behind the wildly successful food blog, *Vegan Yack Attack*, and author of the popular cookbook *Vegan Bowl Attack!*

Jackie has photographed cookbooks for the likes of Jason Wrobel, Happy Herbivore, What the Health, and many other plant-based brands, and is also the Sweet Treats columnist for *VegNews* magazine, where she develops amazing vegan dessert recipes for the masses. Her work has been featured on KTLA, *SELF* magazine, *Thrive* magazine, PureWow, BuzzFeed, and more.

When she is not contemplating her next creation, or obsessing over vegan mac 'n cheese, she enjoys traveling, crafting, eating with friends, and spending time in the outdoors.

INDEX